D0927236

WHEN LOVE
PREVAILS

WHEN LOVE PREVAILS

A Sikh Woman Finds Christ

NARINDAR MEHAT
with
MARGARET WARDELL

OM
publishing

First published in the UK 1998 by Paternoster Press

03 02 01 00 99 98   7 6 5 4 3 2 1

Paternoster Press is an imprint of Paternoster Publishing,
P.O. Box 300, Carlisle, Cumbria CA3 0QS

British Library Cataloguing in Publication Data

A catalogue record for this book is available from the
British Library.

ISBN 0-85078-288-1

Typeset by WestKey Ltd, Falmouth, Cornwall
Printed in Great Britain by Mackays of Chatham PLC, Kent

CONTENTS

ACKNOWLEDGEMENTS

We are grateful to a number of people who have helped us in the production of this book. In particular to Martina Platten who did some of the preparatory work and Maria Frindle and Andrew Becker who audio-typed a veritable mountain of tapes.

Several people read an early draft of the manuscript. They include Revd and Mrs Alan Thomas, Rt. Revd and Mrs Howell Davies, Revd and Mrs Douglas Field, Revd Duncan McMann, Mrs Joan Ditch and Mrs Enid Dansey. They had all been involved in Narindar's life at various points and the accuracy of their memories was a great asset.

Special thanks too must go to Hilary Warner who painstakingly read and commented on both earlier and later drafts of the book and Heather Pike who read the Appendix and suggested some helpful improvements. Pauline Page was a great help to Margaret in getting to grips with a new word-processing programme.

Many thanks to Jenny Taylor, our editor, who was always ready with suggestions and comments and has steered the book through the final processes.

We gratefully acknowledge permission to reproduce Amy Carmichael's poem, 'O for a Passionate Passion for Souls', from *Amy Carmichael of Dohnavur* by Frank Houghton, Published by Dohnavur Fellowship, UK/The Christian Literature Crusade, Fort Washington, PA, USA.

O for a passionate passion for souls,
O for a pity that yearns!
O for the love that loves unto death,
O for the fire that burns!
O for the pure prayer power that prevails,
That pours itself out for the lost!
Victorious prayer in the Conqueror's Name,
O for a *Pentecost*!

1

Introduction

Two Christian friends were praying with me when I heard myself scream, 'Oh God, save me, save me, save me. I will serve you.' As I cried out I saw myself, when still a foetus, running upwards, away from the mouth of my mother's womb. The next moment I sensed myself being born. I seemed to emerge into a vast room and heard a woman crying, 'Oh, it's a girl, it's a girl.' Then everything went strangely quiet. I felt terrified of the unknown world in which I found myself. I didn't want to be part of it.

Next, as Douglas and Catherine Field continued to pray, I saw myself at four or five years old wearing a lovely green coat and with bright ribbons in my hair. I was making patterns with my finger in the dust on the floor. I paused, looked up and saw a shadow pass over me and disappear. Looking back now I feel it was the shadow of almighty God. So I know that He is with me, whatever the situation in which I find myself.

At the same time I was extremely afraid of the evil spirits that seemed to be active in my life. Douglas and Catherine were experienced in confronting these, so I had asked them to come and pray with me. Once or twice in my childhood I had had similar sensations. But now they were more severe. My husband, Sewa, and I were inexperienced in combating such attacks. As we sat in our lounge at bedtime I would say to him, 'Oh, Sewa, I'm frightened. Don't go upstairs. Sit with me while I pray.' But he would simply say, 'Call upon the name of the Lord Jesus. You'll be all right'. Then he would go to bed. After struggling a little longer I would run upstairs to him as fast as I could. As the months passed I began to think, 'Staying downstairs alone is a waste of time. I'm not praying while I'm so scared.'

I had been attending meetings on Friday evenings at Douglas and Catherine's house before I experienced these sensations.

The two of them taught us about the work of the Holy Spirit and we prayed together. So one evening when I went I told everyone how terrified I was of the strange happenings in my house. Immediately the whole group gathered round me and prayed. I returned home calmed but the attacks continued. I was still petrified of sitting in my own lounge so I phoned Douglas and Catherine and they came and prayed for me in the name of Jesus. That's when I experienced the visions of my childhood.

Afterwards the Lord Jesus gave me peace that no guru had ever given me. I thank him from the bottom of my heart for setting me free from the attacks of Satan.

My mother was fifteen and my father seventeen when they married. He was still at school. They knew little about married life when I was conceived soon after the wedding. They lived with my father's parents as is customary in Indian culture. It is also the custom, after a girl has been married for a month or so, for her to return to her own parents' home for an extended visit. My mother's mother had died but her three aunties, although they had their own separate homes in the village, still often came to the family home. When they heard that my mother was pregnant they felt alarmed. They said to each other, 'She's only a little girl. She can't possibly cope with bringing up a baby'. So they tried to terminate the pregnancy in the only way they knew. They heated some water in a large pot on the open fire in the courtyard, poured it into a tin tub and made my mother sit in it. Whenever the water became a little cool, they poured more in from the pot on the fire, to make it as hot as she could possibly bear. They did this on several days. But then my grandfather heard of the aunties' activities. The next time they came to the house he confronted them and yelled, 'Get out! Go away! Don't dare to abort this baby! I want a grandchild!' So this was the origin of my vision of the foetus, running upwards away from the hot water.

As I grew up, my mother would sometimes tell me this story and say, 'Look at you. They tried to make me abort you. If only they knew what a fine young woman you have become.'

2

A Girl Who Wants to Learn!

When I was about four years old I started making a great deal of fuss and repeating, 'I want to go to school! I want to go to school!' The family were puzzled. Village people like them didn't think sending girls to school was important, even though my mother had primary education and her aunt was a teacher.

One day, when my mother could no longer stand the bouts of screaming in which I indulged, she took me to a house in her parents' village. There a family had let out their large downstairs room for a private girls' school, while they lived upstairs. One or two teachers, not necessarily trained, taught the pupils a little reading and writing and simple skills, such as sewing. There was no playground and no opportunity for games. My mother asked them to admit me but they refused because I was not yet five. So we trudged home again. Being under age meant nothing to me so I continued fussing. Eventually, in desperation, my mother took me in her arms and returned to the school. There she said to the teacher, 'She doesn't give me any rest at home because she's insisting on going to school. There's no nursery where I can take her so I'm going to leave her here with you.' All the girls were much older than me, some ten years old, some fifteen. When I arrived they were all learning to cook while I couldn't even tie the string that held up my trousers. But I sat on a bench feeling very proud of myself, though everyone ignored me. I just watched the teacher, who was pockmarked from smallpox, walking round the room with a ruler in her hand. After that I insisted on going every day, just for the morning. There was nothing for me to do there yet it satisfied my childish ego. My mother taught me to read and write at home and I learnt quickly. Her aunt often said to her, 'You should have your daughter educated. She is bright and you mustn't waste her ability even though educating girls isn't the done thing in our families.' She saw it as a way in which I could be free of the restrictions that bound most women in Indian society. But as I look back now I see that, above all, it prepared me to serve God.

I loved my mother dearly and thought her pretty. Her features were rather sharp but they were offset by her lovely, deep brown eyes. She had a fair complexion for an Indian. Of course like most Sikh ladies she never cut her hair. It hung down her back, sometimes in one plait, sometimes in two. On occasion, she would twist it up into a bun. She always dressed well. At home she wore a *salwar kameez*, the typical Punjabi dress for women. This consists of baggy or tight trousers, according to the fashion of the day, and a loose top of the same material, usually knee length. When my mother went out she would wear a sari, a six yard length of material wound round the body in a special way. She owned a number of these outfits in a variety of colours and patterns that I thought most attractive.

Even before I went to school I took an interest in everything my mother did. She yearned for a son and when she became pregnant again she prayed a great deal. In the Sikh religion into which I was born women were taught that when pregnant they should spend more time than usual in prayer. When my mother prayed she would sit cross-legged on a mat. I would sit beside her and listen. One morning, instead of sitting still I spent the time dancing round the room, jumping up and down and disturbing her concentration. She stopped praying and made me stand beside her. Then she said, 'God is almighty, greater than anything we can imagine. He hears prayers and answers and we must honour him by being quiet when we pray.' After that when she prayed I would sit beside her with my hands folded. So I began to experience God's peace when I was very young.

Soon I started to act in ways that are unusual for young girls in Indian society. I loved going to the Sikh gurdwara, which was just outside the village. My mother would dress me up in a beautiful frock, often made of voile, and lace-up shoes with crepe soles. Most children would either stay away from the gurdwara or, if present, hide behind their mothers' backs. But I would run along holding my mother's hand, eager to join in worship.

A high wall surrounded the grounds of the gurdwara. On each side of the gate were small pools of water where we took off our shoes and washed our feet. We left our shoes there. No one would ever steal them. A grey and black tiled path led into the building. A tree of the kind pronounced sacred by Guru Gobind Singh grew just outside its door. We walked round this tree, bowing as we did so. Then, covering our heads, we entered the worship room. There the Guru Granth Sahib, our holy book, had pride of place in the centre front. It rested on a stand, with a richly decorated canopy above. Each person who came into the room knelt before it, touching the floor in front of them with their head and presenting an offering, usually money. Even as a child I understood that we were not bowing to the book itself but to God whom the book represents. So I bowed in awe for I always feared him, even from my earliest days. Often we went alone just to pay our respects to God but on the first day of the month, and on other special occasions, the gurdwara would be full. After paying my respects to the holy book, I would sit on the floor with my mother. Men sat on one side of the room and women and children on the other. The priest would read the scriptures and the congregation would also recite parts of them. I didn't understand a word they said, as the text was in old-fashioned Punjabi, but I felt greatly satisfied at having said something to the gurus. At that age I couldn't distinguish between the gurus, the spiritual teachers of Sikhism, and God. Sometimes I added my own words, usually, 'Oh God, help me.' Though what I needed help for at that age I didn't know. Most of all I liked the *karah prasad*, a special sweet semolina mixture given to each person at the end of the service. Sometimes *akhand path* (a reading of the entire *Ad Granth*), or another service that lasted a day or two, took place. Then I would sing songs in the gurdwara, at the time of the final celebration. I learnt to sing at an early age and particularly liked religious songs. In those days the grown ups encouraged the children to sing in the worship meetings even when they were small. I was about nine at the time.

My family gossiped about God a great deal and I listened to everything they said. I soon started praying by myself. I would ask for childlike things and it seemed that whatever I asked for

I received. My mother, father and grandfather used to give me gifts that other children didn't receive. I thought it was because of my prayers.

My mother's life and conversation made a deep impression on me. She prayed a lot and she loved me dearly. She taught me religious truths, as well as continuing with reading and writing. My childhood was different from all the other children in the village. I used to envy them because they spent their time playing while I was studying.

When I reached my fifth birthday my mother determined to have me educated by trained teachers. There was no government school in my village so she took me to my father's family village. There was no school there either. Eventually my aunt, my father's sister, carried me each day to a school two or three miles away. We followed the wide paths between the fields. Sometimes we met a bullock cart piled high with sugar cane or whatever other crop the farmers were harvesting at the time. My aunt still remembers this. When someone is writing to me she often sends a message saying, 'Have you forgotten how I used to carry you to school every morning?' In the afternoon a boy of about fourteen who lived near us used to bring me home on the cross bar of his bicycle. There were thirty or forty boys in the school but I was the only girl. The teachers were all men too. I wrote on a slate with a pencil made out of a bamboo stick. It was difficult for my mother to explain her motives in sending me there. But by then she had determined she would see me graduate from the university.

My mother would like to have gone on to secondary school herself but her mother died when she was ten or eleven years old. Her father wanted her to stay at home and learn all sorts of domestic duties, as well as knitting and weaving carpets. He thought that if she had these skills he could marry her off quickly. She didn't want me to have the same fate. She instilled in me an independent spirit that has lasted to this day. I believe that is what has brought me so far. I became a Christian against all opposition. I also wanted to serve God and believe the origin of that desire was, unknowingly, the promise I had made in my mother's womb.

I said earlier that my mother married at fifteen and my father at seventeen. My mother was an only daughter and he was an only son. My paternal grandparents wanted their son married with great pomp and show. They were delighted when my mother's family offered their daughter in marriage . Both families were quite wealthy so they arranged a magnificent wedding ceremony. They wanted grandchildren as soon as possible and were thrilled when I was born. I was four and a half before my first brother arrived and I think my elders rather spoilt me.

I remember my father as a young man. He was short in stature for a Punjabi but I thought him handsome. He was darker than my mother with a large face and wide set eyes. Like all Sikh men he wore a beard held in shape by a small piece of net. He always wore a turban, sometimes one colour sometimes another. Otherwise I only ever remember seeing him in western clothes. When he had finished his final year at school he went on to college and gained a BA in maths. Then he trained as a teacher. After his graduation we moved to a small town near Delhi where he was headmaster of a middle school for four or five years. There were plenty of schools in the town. I attended a good private one for girls until I was old enough to go to my father's. There I was able to experience co-education. But my father really longed to be near his own village So we returned to the family home when I was about ten. Again there was no girls' school nearby so I had to go away to one. But, when I was twelve, my parents felt I was old enough to travel to school on my own. So I returned home and cycled daily to a school in a nearby town, using the same sort of paths as those along which my aunt had carried me years before.

All the time my love for God was growing, whether my mother encouraged me or not. I delighted in taking a group of school friends to the gurdwara to sing the gurus' praises. I taught them the songs myself, without the help of any adult. I was only ten or eleven at the time. I also listened carefully to the teaching given in the gurdwara, The priest told us stories of how the gurus conducted their lives. 'God was pleased with their behaviour,' he said, 'and you should try to imitate them in your own lives.'

I also went to Sikh conferences with my mother. Sometimes in our own village, sometimes in a neighbouring one. In such places there is often a big tree with a large brick platform built around it, where the village men gather to talk. Conferences took place there or in the gurdwara in the evenings. Sometimes they lasted all night, so I often went to sleep. But I always wanted to attend them. I liked to be anywhere where I could hear teaching about God. In school I would be the first to sing songs about the gurus. I don't know why I had such longings for God. Perhaps I wanted to know more about a person who was almighty and so much greater than any human being. I certainly was always listening to the stories of what the gurus did and wondering what God was asking of me.

I was always doing things not done by other children of my age, both in the house and at the gurdwara. My grandmother used to laugh and say, 'I don't know where she's come from. She's so different from most girls of her age.' Many people used to wonder why I acted as I did. My mother continued to teach me about God. She wanted me to go on worshipping him and asking him for what I wanted, particularly for education. She used to tell me that education would bring the freedom women in our society needed. She was very liberated herself for those days though she couldn't have the privileges she was giving me. Our families were well off but backward in their views about educating girls. My father's sister, the one who carried me to school, had never gone there herself. He had many privileges though, going to boarding school in a nearby town and then further afield to college. He had control of his own money for paying his expenses too, a thing unheard of, even for most boys, in those days. But my mother had to be the dutiful daughter-in-law, looking after the home and family. Even though her auntie had become a teacher, my mother's father only allowed her primary education. She rebelled against it sometimes but mostly she had to toe the line. She did not want me ever to be in the same situation. She sometimes said, 'Once you are educated and have a good job you will never need to depend on anyone.' But she forgot that we cannot always manage our lives on our own. We need God.

3

Life in the Punjab

There is one God.
He is the supreme truth.
He is the Creator,
Is without fear and without hate.
He, the omnipresent
Pervades the universe.
He is not born
Nor does he die to be born again.
By his grace shalt thou worship him.
Before time itself, there was truth.
When time began to run its course he was the truth.
Even now, he is the truth
and evermore shall truth prevail.

This is the most sacred of all Sikh scriptures and, when I began to say my own prayers, this is where I started. I usually went up onto the flat roof of our house, covered my head and sat cross-legged on the floor. I handled my *gutka*, the small prayer book, with great reverence. I always wrapped it in a beautiful cloth and frequently bowed to it because it was the word of God.

Our house was made of cement and brick. It was so large that sometimes when a person was in one corner of it the rest of the family didn't know where he or she was. The largest room downstairs was the sitting room where we entertained guests. In front of it was a large verandah. We used to eat our meals there in summertime. In winter in the Punjab it is too cold to do so.

Upstairs was one large room that no one could enter except to study. Shelves full of books in Punjabi, Urdu, Hindi and English lined the walls. The most treasured ones were in glass fronted bookcases. Many of them were religious but there were also a large number on ethics, history, mathematics and other subjects. My mother also read novels that she kept there. I spent much time in that room and so did my father. We would often discuss matters of mutual interest together. We sometimes joked that we had enough books to open a lending library. A large table and several cane chairs occupied the centre of the room. A bed stood near one wall. In India most rooms contain a bed as people rest after lunch in the hot weather. The only other person allowed in the room was my Alsatian dog, Romi. I loved him dearly and he loved me and accompanied me everywhere he possibly could. Pictures hung on the walls of our house, some of them of the gurus, others family photographs, including one of my grandfather in army uniform.

In front of the house was an earthen courtyard, surrounded by walls six feet high. The gate in one side was even higher, seven feet or more. The person who built it determined that no passer-by should see what we were doing. When he was seven or eight years old my father had planted two neem trees in the yard. By the time I was born they were huge. When he was older he also planted sunflowers. My mother cultivated guava and pomegranate trees and a flower-bed in which she usually grew fragrant white flowers. Birds nested in the trees, especially parrots in a rich variety of colours. They flew hither and thither across the courtyard all day long.

At the back of the house were two small kitchens and beyond them a small yard where we had our hand pump. In the evening my grandfather brought our two buffaloes home and milked them there. During the day they grazed in an area some distance from the house. Buffalo milk is rich and creamy. We also kept cows, goats and hens.

From the flat roof where I prayed I could see for miles. Our house was on the edge of the village so from one side I saw fields stretching to the horizon, from the other the village houses. There were about two hundred and fifty of them, many with mud walls and thatched roofs. Most people were landowners. My grandfather was the chief one; a sort of squire.

When I looked at the nearby fields, I could see farmers ploughing, sowing or reaping, according to the season. They cultivated wheat, barley, sugar cane, maize, cotton and many kinds of fruit and vegetables. After harvesting whatever crop was ripe the farmers put aside what they needed for their own food. They piled the rest into oxcarts and took it to markets in the neighbouring towns. Non-landowners often leased a few acres from the richer farmers. At harvest time the landlord would come for his share of the crops, just as in Bible times.

From the flat roof I also saw women looking after cattle or taking out food for their menfolk. Usually this would consist of chapatis, a small earthenware dish of vegetable curry and a drink of lassi. In Britain we know lassi as buttermilk. The women would wrap the food in a cloth to keep it warm and carry it on their heads or under their arms. Sometimes I saw women walking to and from the well with pots on their heads. The richer members of the community did not have to go the well. They had hand pumps in their own yards as we did.

Our farm had sixty or seventy acres, a large area in those days. My mother's grandfather had lived in Burma for several years and still had businesses there so her family were quite wealthy.

I also heard a variety of sounds from the rooftop: someone shouting for a family member or an animal that had strayed; someone singing at their work. Sometimes I heard tick, tick, tick as the white oxen walked in a circle round and round the well. This turned the wheel to which were attached a series of buckets. When it was down in the well the bucket filled with water, but as it reached the top it spilled its water into the channel leading from the well to irrigate the fields. Sometimes, in the evening, I heard the sound of the peacock. It looks beautiful when it fans out its tail feathers and 'dances' but it has a raucous voice.

My village is called Sultanpur, and is in the Punjab, equidistant from the cities of Jullundur and Ludhiana. When we needed something like clothes, cutlery or other factory-made goods we had an hour's bus ride to one or the other place. We produced most of our own food on the farm.

True Sikhs believe God is one; nevertheless, village people often worship spirits as Hindus do. In our village one such spirit was called Baba Balak Nath. Many villagers worshipped him. Baba is the name given to a saint. Legend says that he began to do miracles when he was only a child. Pictures of him show a round-faced boy of about twelve, wrapped in an animal skin. My mother only started to believe in him when I was about seventeen years old, although my grandfather had been worshipping him for several years.

After my father emigrated to Britain my mother became ill. One day she was sitting under a tree in our front yard when a *pundit* happened to pass by. He read palms and told fortunes. The front gate was open and he looked in and saw my mother. 'Are you all right?' he asked, 'You look disappointed.' She was feeling extremely ill. When she looked at him she knew he was a fortune-teller and said, 'I don't know what's the matter with me.' He replied, 'I'm going to tell you about Baba Balak Nath. Make a promise that you will give him something if he heals you. One sick person promised to go and visit him at his temple in the hills and she was healed.' That transformed my mother. She regained strength and began to have great faith in the spirit of Baba Balak Nath. She used to make pilgrimages of two or three days to reach the temple where she could worship his pictures. Like most of his followers she wore a three-sided cross and burned incense in his honour. Every time anything was needed in the home she prayed to him as well as the ten gurus.

My mother also bargained with the deities. If one of them answered her prayers she would distribute sweets to all who came to the house, not just family members. She would also go out on to the street and give them to everyone who passed by. Many villagers did something like this when their prayers were answered. People who received the sweets thanked the deity whom they believed had responded.

At night in the village we used to hold meetings on the flat roofs of the houses where we sang hymns. As Christians greet each other with the words, 'Victory to Jesus' or 'Glory to the Saviour' so the villagers used to say, 'Glory and victory to the spirit.' The faith of the whole community grew, and our family's faith too. Many villages in the Punjab are in the grip of Baba Balak Nath's spirit. His worship is spreading among Sikhs and Hindus in Britain too. Temples are being built in his honour, including one quite near our home in Wolverhampton. My father also began to worship him after we came to England. My mother had tremendous influence on us three children so we believed in Baba Balak Nath too. The spirit had complete hold over us. I used to have nightmares of him running after me with a stick. His power over me was only broken when I turned to Jesus Christ.

At the gurdwara or at Sikh conferences we heard the stories of the gurus, their sacrifices, the miracles they performed, their life style. Guru Nanak was the founder of Sikhism and we heard stories of his travels all over India as well as his teaching. The storytellers spoke with such a zing and enthusiasm that the words went deep into the soul. In the Sikh conferences the teachers always exhorted us to imitate the gurus in our conduct. The musicians told their stories in song. I used to love these conferences and always begged my mother to take me. If she said, 'No,' I would cry and then she gave in, though when I arrived there I often fell asleep. Nevertheless, I genuinely wanted to learn more about God.

Sometimes we went to Hindu conferences. There we might see a drama about the life of the God Krishna for instance. It would continue night after night. I always wanted to go but often my mother wouldn't let me, saying, 'You are too little and you have to have some sleep so that you are ready for school in the morning.'

My mother was good to needy people. We had a girl working in our house whom she had rescued from ill-treatment. She came from a poor family. Her mother had died and her father didn't want to keep her with him, so he put her in the care of her maternal aunt and uncle in our village. But they were cruel. Often they refused to speak to her for days and deprived her of food and clothes. My mother used to feed her, buy her clothes and look after her health. If ever we children mistreated her, my mother would reprimand us severely. The girl looked after our chickens, did the washing and all the other normal duties in the home.

We were a small family. I felt loved by every member of it. I was four years and ten months old when my next brother was born. So I was an only child for several years. My uncle, my mother's brother, adored me. He used to cut my hair, dress me in clothes he liked and take me everywhere on his bicycle. Sikh girls don't usually have their hair cut but I was a special child and treated differently from most children. My mother brought me up in quite a western way. I wore short pants and shirts until I was seven or eight years old. Then I graduated to a dress and long trousers. I didn't start wearing a *salwar kurta*, the usual dress for Punjabi women, till I was thirteen or fourteen. My family, being rich, lived luxurious lives. They spared no expense to make our surroundings beautiful. I had a lovely childhood but I was well aware of the poverty all around and that touched my heart. It also turned me to God more than ever, for I realized he was the only one who could really help the poor.

4

Disappointment

Even before I reached secondary school I knew about the Sikh
doctrine of reincarnation. My mother had told me that we had
to go through 8.4 million cycles of births and deaths before we
would win salvation. Achieving salvation meant becoming one
spirit with God. If we had lived a good life we would be reborn
next time to a higher position in society. If we were faithful in
meditating on God's name the number of our cycles of reincarnation might even be reduced. If we were not faithful we might
come back as an animal or even an insect. I knew I had not
always been good and was terrified that I might come back as
a snake or some other lower form of life. Sometimes I thought I
should run away to the hills like Naina Devi so that I might find
salvation as she did. Naina Devi's shrine was in the hills to the
north of us. Her followers journeyed there to offer food and
flowers to her idol and plead with her to answer their prayers.
She was supposed to have been a young girl who lived locally.
One day she ran away to the hills because she was unhappy.
People say she went beneath the ground and became a deity.
Some village people worshipped her. Many times, even as a
child, I thought, 'If I commit suicide the cycle of births and
deaths will start a bit earlier. Then I will be with God sooner.'
Right from my childhood I constantly heard my elders talking
about reincarnation. They feared it, so I did too. The idea of
getting out of the cycle preyed on my mind constantly. Everyone said there was no way I could do so. But I tried just the same.
I would go anywhere to find out more about it; to Sikh gurdwaras, Hindu temples and the shrines of the spirits. I had a deep
thirst to find out more about the supernatural. When I asked my
mother, 'How can I get out of this cycle?' she would say, 'Well,
all the maharishees, saints and deities went into the jungles and
meditated day and night. Only then did they receive salvation.'
She did not know enough to put me on the path to the deeper

spiritual truths I was seeking. But she did her best and shared all she could. Her prayer life was consistent and because of that mine became consistent when I was quite young.

It began when I was about ten years old. I used to pray over and over again that God would give me education. My other constant prayer was that I would have salvation. Unbeknown to my family I was concentrating on God all the time. Most mornings and evenings after I had done my homework I used to go to the top of the house and pray as I had seen my parents do. Praying meant reciting out of the *gutka*. I knew of no other way. The *gutka* contains a selection of the choicest prayers from the Guru Granth Sahib. Sikhs use it at home much as Christians might use a copy of the Psalms or the New Testament rather than the entire Bible. The complete Guru Granth Sahib is a large, unwieldy book and a family who owns a copy must keep it in a special place and use it with great reverence. They must not carry it around in a casual way. When I had finished my recitation on the rooftop, I prayed that God would give me education.

When he was at home, my father would often read the stories of the gurus aloud and he and my mother would discuss them. I would listen. I had an excellent memory and very little of what I heard escaped me. I remember my mother once said, 'Don't talk about anyone in front of Narindar. She remembers everything and goes and repeats it to the person concerned.'

Gradually I began to spend more time in prayer and to discipline myself to sit more reverently. If my thoughts wandered I would force myself to refocus on God over and over again. Prayer became increasingly important to me. I also tried to discipline my daily life, being concerned not to tell even a white lie. If I did do wrong I confessed my sin over and over again. I thought God would answer my prayers if I did. Once, when I was about fourteen years old, I visited a Sikh temple and promised that I would read the complete *gutka* a particular number of times. And I did so, day and night, all because I feared God so much. Paradoxically I also loved him.

At the same time I worried about the poverty-stricken people I used to see at the roadside. So many of the things about the lifestyle permitted by my culture troubled me too. I heard stories about the joint family system right from my childhood. When a girl married she had to leave her family and go and live in her husband's village. I hated that. She had to live with her in-laws because they had the land in their hands. Usually they didn't allow their daughter-in-law any freedom. Often her mother-in-law would beat her and force her to do all the household work: washing, cleaning, cooking and making the cow dung cakes that were used for fuel when dried. When I saw the girl from a lower caste doing all the menial tasks in our home I used to think, 'How come I have all the best? Why can't she have all that I do?' I also felt disturbed because the traditions of our culture did not permit a girl to remarry if her husband died. Nor could a husband and wife divorce if they did not get on together. My mother's aim in seeing that I received education was to set me free from the traditions which bound women in our society. I prayed for that too.

I used to make promises to myself as a child, such as, 'When I grow up, I'm going to do something to help the poor people. I don't want much money like my parents and grandparents have, but I want salvation.' I had a genuine compassion for the poor but I also hoped that through good works I would find salvation.

When I was twelve or thirteen I decided to become a doctor so I worked extremely hard and did well at school. I gained admission to the pre-medical course at a government college. Then I needed a place in the college hostel. Places were limited however and people in high positions had approached the college in private to secure a place for their daughters. Most of those from the villages, like myself, faced disappointment. All the vacancies were filled by the time we applied. Some of them arranged to board in private homes but my family wouldn't allow me to do so. They had heard of girls who did this being sexually abused and even raped, so they wouldn't trust anyone else to look after me. Most parents also worried that their girls might meet boys, unless they were living either in a hostel or their own home. If society knew that a girl had had any contact at all with boys, then the parents would experience difficulty in finding a marriage partner for her. So I had to give up the idea of being a doctor. I felt deeply disappointed. Even today my heart aches when I think about it. If I had studied medicine, how much more I could have done for the Lord.

I hadn't told my mother why I wanted to be a doctor. If I had said it was in order to serve the poor, she would have put a stop to it. I grieved, because I believed that, as a doctor, I would have had the freedom to do what I liked with my life.

However, despite this disappointment, I was basically happy. My family loved me and I loved them. I knew their chief concern was to give me the best start in life that they possibly could and I felt deeply grateful for that.

5

College

When I was fifteen I left school and went to college. The uneducated village people didn't approve. They thought cities were places of moral danger for girls. When girls went away from home to study they used to say, 'She's going to run away with someone.' In addition, people who belonged to my caste, the Jat Sikhs, would rather spend money on buying land than on educating their daughters. But my grandfather had been in the army, my father was well educated and my mother quite liberated even though she had only primary education. They put up with all the criticism that came their way.

I went to the Khalsa College for women in the district of Ludhiana. There I studied for a degree in History, Economics and English. There were about two hundred students and we lived in a hostel. First year students shared a room with two or three other girls but more senior ones had their own room. The services of such people as the *dhobi* (washerman), the dry-cleaner and the tailor were available whenever we needed them. The hostel had its own prayer room where girls could go and read the Guru Granth Sahib and pray. Though it was a Sikh college, the principal was a Christian. I think her faith must have been only nominal, because she never spoke of it. However she did give all new students a copy of the Bible. Mine had a green cover. My parents would never have sent me to a Christian college, for they thought all Christians were low caste. Even when I was only three or four years old, my elders told me never to go near Christians. They said that missionaries paid people to become Christian. Since becoming one myself, I realize our people didn't understand that Christians look after the downtrodden. If the people they helped became Christians as a result that was fine.

As I scanned the Bible the principal had given me I found I didn't understand much of it. So I put it on a shelf at home. I didn't look at it again. However, one day, I walked into the college library looking for some interesting books to read in my spare time. I don't know why, but I went over to the religious section and took a book of Old Testament stories from the shelf. It was a large book with lots of pictures. One showed Moses praying to God, who was enveloped in a great cloud of light. This was the first time in my fifteen years that I understood that God is light. I was so interested that I went to the library again and took out other Old Testament stories. The librarian looked at me but he didn't say anything. I felt deeply satisfied as I read them, but that was all. None of them gripped me as much as the story of Moses and the burning bush. I didn't go on to the New Testament. However one thing was clear to me: God was light. This concept changed my life. I puzzled repeatedly about the right way to approach God. No one knew the struggle that was going on inside me.

I started to pray differently. I began by reciting the prayers from the Sikh holy books. When Sikhs have finished reading their Scriptures they sit down and pray freely. They praise God and thank him for blessings they have received. I did this, but then went on to bring the cloud of light before my eyes. I refused to focus on anything else. As I concentrated on this, I would tell God, 'I want to worship and serve you alone.' I don't know where I learned the word 'service'. Nobody had ever talked about it at home, at school or at college.

When I went home for the holidays my life took a new turn. My liking for God had turned into love for him. Something inside me used to draw me to the top of the house, where I had so often prayed before. I prayed with joy and excitement instead of fear. I still recited out of the *gutka*, which consists mostly of praise to God, but afterwards I brought the cloud of light before my eyes. I had not heard of anybody else experiencing such a thing or teaching about it but I continued to do it without telling anyone.

Until I experienced this, my reciting of the Sikh books and my praying consisted of asking for gifts or blessings or telling God all the troubles of my youth. Now after reading the Scriptures I used to say, 'I want to serve you, God.' I had often seen the priests in the gurdwara reciting out of the holy books and I thought this was service to God. I used to think what a wonderful life they had and long to be in their place. I knew I couldn't because it wasn't considered appropriate for girls of my background. I was privileged to have many good things, especially a college education; yet I was asking God to make it possible for me to be a priest! I concentrated my prayers on this for the next two years, to the exclusion of anything else.

My dependency upon God was increasing. Seeing him as a cloud of light had made me realize he was a real God and I felt excited. Now, as I spent time at home on the roof reciting and praying to the light, something strange started happening. I would sense an aroma around me; an aroma of flour fried in oil; that of an Indian sweet known as *parshad*. It is referred to in the Bible, in Leviticus. When I began to smell the *parshad* I would go sniffing everywhere. Where was it coming from? I would shout to my mother from the top of the house, 'Are you making some *parshad*?' 'No, I'm not', she would say. So I didn't tell her what was happening. I became so fond of the aroma that whenever possible I would take up my *gutka* and go and pray. And sure enough the aroma would be there again! I loved it and would start praising God and asking him to allow me to serve him.

My mother was still an ardent worshipper of the gurus and the spirits. Sometimes I had to stand with her before the picture of a guru and bow. At other times I would go with her to distribute sweets. While doing so I would be thinking, 'It's all very well giving such things in the name of Baba Balak Nath or some other spirit but what about God? Where is he in all this?' Nevertheless I would accompany her for the sake of peace. I don't know why, but I never told her about the aroma or that I wanted to be a priest. Perhaps it was because I already felt disappointed about not studying medicine. So I withdrew into myself. I was angry with God too. 'Why wasn't I allowed to go into medicine?' I cried. I determined that the question of what I was to do instead should be between God and me. I had so much wanted to look after needy people when I was in school. How was I going to do so now?

Another question I asked was, 'Why wasn't I born a boy?' I felt that girls didn't have the opportunities boys did. Girls had to stay quietly in the house, learning all the home skills such as sewing and cooking, until they married. Then after their marriage they had to put this into practice in their husband's home. It was such a restricted life. If I had gone into medicine, I would have gained the freedom to do what I wanted.

Part of me was running away from the traditions of society. I saw its evils and wanted to give my life to doing good deeds. Mixed up with my desire to serve God was the thought that the more good deeds I did the more sure of gaining salvation I would be. Yet I also wanted to know more about God so that I could come closer to him. I frequently heard holiness talked about in the Sikh temples and in my home. We were taught that the way to achieve it was to avoid stealing, fighting, drinking, smoking and other such vices. It was a matter of conduct rather than inner attitude. So I made it my goal to achieve holiness if that would bring salvation. To be holy I had to be thoughtful and alert at all times. I became absolutely obsessed with the idea of holiness. I envied people like Naina Devi. They had supernatural powers and so were close to God. I wanted those powers. If ever I made any wrong statement or did something wrong I would spend days and days repenting. When I first became a Christian I did the same thing, focusing on holiness so much that I would fast and pray for days for the wrong I had done. But I didn't tell any one.

I was, of course, away from home now in term time but in the holidays I used to think through what I was going to do for God. But I wasn't coming to any conclusions. I had no one to guide me. All I knew was that when I grew up I wanted to do something for God to redress the injustice in the world. I would look after the poor and needy. These ideas dominated my mind. I agonized about the women's life in the villages. I wanted to look after battered wives, girls whose parents didn't look after them and daughters-in-law being abused by their mothers-in-law.

A few families in the village were not short of anything but I could count them on my fingers. Most people just made ends meet. They had small farms and could eat three meals a day but had little left for anything else. In some families the husbands drank the money away. Sometimes people would borrow money from their richer neighbours until harvest time. When people asked my mother for a loan on that basis she sometimes wouldn't give them one because she knew they couldn't repay. Some people borrowed from moneylenders who charged enormous rates of interest. Often people struggled all their lives without ever being able to pay off the loan.

There was a special area in the village where the people who worked with animal hides lived. Curing animal hides was despised work, considered fit only for the lowest of the low. The people who did it were extremely poor. Their houses were made of mud, and badly maintained. They contained no furniture except a bed or two. Only they used the well in that area. They didn't come into the Sikh gurdwara but stood just outside where people would give them food from the *langar* (the gurdwara's dining room). They worked in the landowners' fields or as building labourers, often on a day-to-day basis. They might receive their wages in goods rather than money. Some days they had no work. Sometimes those who were sick just died because they couldn't afford medical treatment. I remember the big pond in that area. I used to see a woman sitting beside it, under a tree. She was half-naked and obviously undernourished. The sight of her used to break my heart.

A village woman lived a terrible life. As a little girl she would have to do all the duties of the household and look after the animals on the farm. She wore tatty clothes and just went on from day to day eating three meals. She spent her time dreaming about when she would marry. It was the only dream a village girl had. Yet, when she did marry, her husband and in-laws would rule her life just as her parents had. I didn't see anything different in a woman's life from the time she started walking till she was on her deathbed. The whole of her life was drudgery, drudgery, drudgery. My heart used to break. But the more it broke the more I prayed for them.

After obtaining my BA degree I went on to study for an MA in modern history at Chandigarh university. Here there were four hostels for girls and some for boys. According to Indian custom we were kept well away from each other. Chandigarh is the capital of the Punjab and is a modern city, built after independence from Britain.

One day in the village, one of my schoolteachers from long ago happened to walk by our house. My mother was standing at the gate. They started to talk together as people do in the villages. He said, 'I remember a little girl who used to come to our school from this village a long time ago. I don't know what happened to her but I feel somehow she's from this house.' On hearing this my mother invited him in and gave him a drink. They continued to talk. She didn't tell the man it was her daughter he was talking about. 'I've often wondered what she's doing now,' he said, 'She was a bright kid.' So my mother said, 'Oh, yes, she's at the university now.' 'The one who came to school wearing a coat?' 'Yes, that's the one.' 'The coat marked me out, because most village children didn't have one and the villagers used to talk about me. I was the only girl who went to university for ten or fifteen miles around.

While I was at university I met some nuns who were serving God among the poor and needy. In Chandigarh city we rarely saw poor people but the nuns knew where they lived and tried to meet their needs of housing, clothing, food and so on. I admired their work, so when I went home for the next holiday I said to my mother, 'I want to be a nun.' She wouldn't let me. Instead she began desperately looking for a husband for me. She certainly didn't want me to be a nun.

In India young people do not usually choose their own marriage partners. Their parents arrange to marry them to whomever they consider suitable. As it happened, Sewa's father had just come to India from Wolverhampton, where the family lived, to look for a bride for Sewa. One of his relatives told him about me so he came to our house to see my mother. They decided to see if I would agree. By this time my father had emigrated to Britain so my mother wrote to him at once and he went to see Sewa. Sewa's parents soon agreed to the marriage. My mother then went to a Hindu priest to see if the match was a good one. Hindu priests foretell the future through astrology. He said, 'Oh, yes, it's a brilliant match'. So she went ahead with the wedding arrangements. Actually this marriage was not all right because I was a devout Sikh and Sewa was an agnostic Sikh, but nobody asked God about it. However, now, looking back I can see God turned my mother's wrong into his right.

After I had finished my exams and even before I knew I had passed, we all joined my father in England. Though I did not know it then, it was the beginning of a chain of events that led to me finding the God I had sought for so long.

6

Marriage and Emigration

I felt quite calm about my first plane flight and looked forward to seeing my father again. On the other hand the idea of marriage didn't appeal to me. It would be hard to serve God when married. I still wanted to be free from the traditions of my family and society that disapproved of a girl being independent. Maybe in England I could find a job and pursue my own interests.

When I arrived in Britain I had no time to think any more about the possibilities. The Mehat family met us at Heathrow airport. Sewa seemed very young. After all he was only just twenty-one. Sewa's father, whom I had met in India, spoke to my father and then asked me if we had had a good journey. His mother put a gold ring on my finger. Sewa and I just said, 'Hello,' to each other. His mother appeared to be a typical Asian mother-in-law. Her clothes and behaviour were old-fashioned. Later I discovered that the older generation of Indians in Britain were more traditional than those in India. Mrs Mehat made it clear that she would be in charge of my future once I married. I knew that meant going to live with her until we could have a place of our own. It was a tradition I was willing to obey if she was kind and undemanding.

My father had borrowed a van to carry us and our luggage to the home that he had prepared for us in Gravesend. Sewa and his family went back to Wolverhampton. My first impressions of London, as we drove through it, were negative. So many buildings cheek by jowl with each other and such crowds of people! I felt England was not for me. My father lived in a terraced house with three bedrooms. He had decorated the lounge tastefully. Behind it was a dining room and a large kitchen. However, after being accustomed to our house in India, I thought this one very small. The outside seemed dull too. In India we painted the outside of our houses in bright colours as well as the inside. There were small gardens at the back and front. I didn't like living in a house like every other house in the street.

When we arrived I said to my mother, 'I don't like the Mehats.' Before we left India she and I had decided that if I didn't like the family, or Sewa or his mother, I wouldn't have to marry him. This was a liberated view. In traditional Indian society a girl didn't normally have such freedom of choice. However, my mother wanted me to be happy and independent. She also agreed that, if I married and found living with my in-laws didn't work, I could come back home.

My father had visited Sewa's family but couldn't make up his mind in one day whether they were a suitable family for me to marry into or not. After further discussion my parents decided to invite Sewa and his whole family to stay with us in Gravesend for a day or two. Then, if I still didn't like them or my parents didn't feel they were a suitable family, my mother and I would return to India. There I would continue to study until some other suitable family could be found.

During the few days the Mehat family were with us, our parents gave Sewa and me time together in a separate room. No one interfered with us. We also went for some walks together. I didn't tell him about my religious views. I felt that was none of his business. But we discussed if and when we might marry. I told him I felt concerned about his family's traditional views of a daughter-in-law. I said that I didn't want to marry a typical Asian husband who expected his wife to be the slave of the family. In India even an educated girl may have to touch her mother-in-law's feet sometimes, as a sign of submission. By the grace of God he had come prepared for whatever my family and I might ask from him. Everything we saw of his family while they were with us commended them to us. His mother seemed much less arrogant and much more loving than she had at the airport. Jat Sikhs are not demonstrative but she did put her arm round me as my own family often did. Sewa and I began to plan what we would do after marrying. Before he and his family left Gravesend my family and I had decided that we would go ahead with the marriage. It took place within a month.

Lots of guests attended the wedding though it wasn't as big or as showy as many Asian ones. Our house was large so we held the reception there. In those days Asian neighbours used to do all the work for the party. They would start preparing Indian sweets and other delicacies weeks beforehand. At many weddings I have attended the men consume much alcohol but at mine we didn't have any at all. Even today when I attend Asian weddings I hate everyone having so much fun while the girl is facing the trauma of leaving her family. I have known the pain of that parting myself. My heart ached at saying goodbye to my own family though I had the security of knowing they were in this country. And they had promised that, if my marriage didn't work out, I could go back to them. Nevertheless I decided to try and make it a success if at all possible. I didn't find it easy.

The Mehat's semi-detached house was in a pleasant part of Wolverhampton but I felt shocked when I saw some of the run-down areas of the city. Sewa had two sisters and a brother and somehow we all fitted into three bedrooms. Sewa and I had one bedroom, his parents another and his sisters the third. His brother had to sleep on a sofa in the lounge. The family were more traditional in dress and behaviour than many families in India. Sewa had lots of relatives in Wolverhampton whom we visited. After a while I didn't want to do that any more because they were traditional too. I tried to be an obedient daughter-in-law, and behaved respectfully towards my mother-in-law. However I still had a great deal of resentment against God in my heart because he hadn't given me what I desired. I wanted to serve him in order to escape the restrictions of Indian society. I didn't want to be tied down the way many Asian brides are even today.

Sewa's father had always wanted a well-educated daughter-in-law. His family were in business and he thought that such a young woman would be an asset. His wife, extended family and community were all against it. They told him she wouldn't be obedient. However he had seen how uneducated people had to suffer when they came to Britain and determined it shouldn't happen in his family. Such was his determination that he persuaded them to give in to all my parents' demands.

In a traditional Asian family the daughter-in-law has to cook, clean, dust, and wash the clothes of the entire family. In short she has to do all the housework. Everyone bosses her. Even the husband's younger brothers and sisters sometimes give their sister-in-law a rough time. I feared this happening to me. However, when Sewa's father had been to see my mother in India she had said, 'My daughter has never done any housework or cooking. She is not going to do any cooking in your house or be a slave to the family. If you want someone who will be, you had better look elsewhere.' So when I arrived in my in-laws' home Sewa's mum looked after me for quite a long time. She said to me, 'You haven't done any work in your mother's home so I'm not going to ask you to do anything here. We're only a small family and I don't go out to work so I can still do the cooking and cleaning.' I felt relieved not to be subjected to family pressure like so many Asian brides. Instead I had the freedom for which I longed.

In any case, I spent three of the first six months with my mother as is traditional for a new bride. After that I started teaching so I was away from home for most of the day. Only when Sewa and I bought our own house did his mother teach me to cook. I only became truly interested in cooking and doing housework when I became a Christian Then I wanted to serve people. Before that I was happy to have others serve me.

Our relatives worried a great deal when Sewa and I decided to live alone in our own house. In those days the Asian community looked on such an action as dishonouring to the family. Couples usually stayed with in-laws until they had children and even children's children. Sewa's father also worried because we were going to live in a 'white' area. He had come to Britain in 1952 and used to tell me about Asian men who had gone to live with English women. Sometimes English men, who were jealous of them, beat them up. Only two or three Asians lived in one area so they couldn't defend themselves. My father-in-law seemed almost more worried for us than for his own family. He didn't stand in the way of us having our own home but he had all sorts of fears about our moving out of the Punjabi community. He told us we should have two phones and get in touch with the family if anything went wrong. My parents-in-law did not worry about our managing financially. By that time I was teaching and Sewa had a good job. They just worried about our safety.

However, we refused to listen to anyone and within a few months of being married we moved into our own house. I now think, looking back, that it was the right thing. If we had stayed with the family we wouldn't have had the freedom to search for God that I had desired from childhood. At the time we moved I had actually gone away from God but he answered my childhood prayers just the same.

At first we lived in a house that belonged to Sewa's father. However it was in an Asian area and our neighbours expected me to be a traditional daughter-in-law. Most of them were totally illiterate. They came from Sewa's mother's village so they thought I was their daughter-in-law as well, and that they could walk over me. They tried to tell me that I ought to wear a *salwar kurta*, not western clothes. They would call out to one another across the street if they wanted to borrow food or other items. Neither Sewa nor I liked this. Within a year we sold that house and moved to Sedgley, on the edge of the city, and right out of the Asian scene. Sewa and I had become one in attitudes and ideas. Our temperaments and expectations of life were similar. We consider our marriage a lifelong commitment to each other. Even when we initially have a difference we quickly listen to and appreciate the other's point of view. We discuss a matter until we come to an agreement about it. Even in those early days Sewa helped at home. We might cook together in the kitchen or, while I was cooking, he would do the vacuuming or clean the windows. Most Asian men would never dream of doing housework. I helped him in the garden; perhaps filling the black bags as he pulled up the weeds; or putting in plants alongside him. We made every effort to grow in understanding of each other. We found ourselves alike in so many matters. When it came to decorating the house we found we liked the same wallpaper patterns and agreed easily about the furniture we needed. We became increasingly happy together. It surprised us at first, as he had been brought up in the West and I in India. However he had developed a liking for British ways, and I had lived away from home among people having more western attitudes. I believe the Lord brought us together.

We settled down in our new home and our lives went smoothly for many years. But I soon discovered that society had the same values as it had in India. People were selfish, greedy and lacked concern for others. This made me angry with God. He had not given me what I had asked for so I stopped reading his praises out of the Sikh holy books and turned away from the religious life completely. I was content to be free from the restrictions of Asian society but in rebellion against God. Sewa did not care for society's values either so we became equal partners in every way, happy in each other's company.

As Sewa and I continued getting our home together we made friends with many English young people. We had no Asian friends except for one girl whom I had known in India. We lived completely in the English community, inviting English friends home and visiting their homes in return. Although we did not know it, God was preparing us for the work he had for us to do one day.

We hadn't made an absolute break from the Asian community. We still went to visit our families. However they couldn't understand our ways and we were angry because they wouldn't try to do so. We felt we had everything we needed; a home, good jobs, no shortage of money and a life of our own. Sometimes we would go to see a film or have a meal in a restaurant. We were secure and happy but forgot God. For eight or nine years I didn't pray. I didn't tell Sewa about my resentment against God because he was never interested in talking about God.

Before I even came to this country my father had been taking *The Times Educational Supplement*. When I arrived I applied to the Department of Education and Science and my degree was verified. I applied to teach History in a secondary school, but when I went round it I felt it was not my cup of tea. The girls were mostly bigger than me and when I heard about the discipline problems I was frightened. One girl had actually threatened a teacher with a knife. So after arriving in Wolverhampton, I began to look around for a post in a primary school.

Everyone said that graduates from India couldn't get jobs straight away but must do a fifteen-month training course. I wasn't prepared to do any more courses, so I stayed at home for about three months. I felt so bored. I had nothing to do except watch television. I had no friends in England. Having been accustomed to being out and about all day, I didn't enjoy being confined to the house.

I was still praying at that time, so I beseeched Baba Balak Nath to find me work. I also wrote many letters of application One day I answered an advertisement from the Birmingham Education Authority. It said that if I was a young graduate I didn't need any more training. The Authority would train me. I went for an interview with them. When I entered the room where the interview was to take place I saw there were a great number of people waiting for me. They were sitting round a large table. But I wasn't scared. I had just finished at university and I felt very sure of myself. I returned home feeling I had acquitted myself well. Within a day or two they wrote offering me a job. I started work in a Birmingham primary school in January 1969. The headmaster had created a very happy atmosphere and I never heard anyone talking against him. When I first went I wondered if I would be able to handle difficult situations, but he put me with a Miss Morgan, a very experienced teacher, and told me just to watch. I did this for about three months. The class was multiracial, though Muslims predominated. Miss Morgan was a small, round-faced Welsh lady in her forties and the headmaster thought highly of her. She was a skilled teacher and on a personal level showed me genuine love. She was calm and patient and an excellent disciplinarian.

Then suddenly her uncle died and she left me in charge of the top infants class for two weeks. The headmaster inspected it often and at the end of that time recommended to the education authority that I be employed straight away. Most of the Asian teachers in Birmingham schools had had teaching experience in India. I was the only one who hadn't. I told one or two Asian graduates and they were angry and jealous because they hadn't been treated in the same way.

I spent two years teaching in Birmingham and then I moved to a primary school in Wolverhampton. At first I taught the reception class and later top infants. Again it was a multiracial school. All the teachers were young except one or two. At first I joined the crowd and was one with them. On Friday evenings we would often go out for a meal or a drink. We enjoyed the night life at clubs and pubs. Sewa always went with me. I wouldn't go alone. It was a joyous kind of life at the time, though in my heart of hearts I knew it wasn't really me. I just went along with the crowd for something to do. I wanted to know what life was like in Britain and this seemed a way to discover. I had set myself the goal of finding happiness. Little did I know that I was looking in the wrong places.

7

A Family Crisis

For several years nothing disturbed the serenity of our lives. We had everything we desired; a comfortable home, interesting jobs, financial security and plenty of friends. However we still had no desire to turn to God. I only attended the gurdwara for weddings or other special occasions.

One summer holiday we went to stay with my parents, who had moved to Dartford. A few days after we arrived, my mother began complaining of a severe headache and said her left hand wasn't working properly. She became so ill that we rushed her to Dartford hospital. They said she must have a scan. In those days the smaller hospitals didn't have the facilities for this, so they sent her to a London hospital. My father went with her. When he came home afterwards he broke the news that she had a brain tumour. 'She needs an operation at once. Even then she may not live.'

My mother had spent her life looking after the family and the home. Her whole life had revolved round my two brothers and me. I was particularly close to her. I had never known any unhappiness, suffering or stress of any kind. Now I felt as though my world was collapsing around me. I dreaded the thought of the operation but realized that without it my mother would die.

Though I had not turned to God for years I began praying. I remembered how he used to help me in India and reminded him of that. I prayed throughout the night as they were operating. 'Please God, make my mum live. If I lose her, my heart will break,' I told him, 'She has been my pillar all through my life.' I took out my *gutka* and recited from it and then began pleading repeatedly, 'O Father God, don't let my mother die!'

My father went to the hospital the next morning and came back to tell us that she had survived and he had seen her. I felt intense relief. When he suggested I visit her too, I was eager to do so. When we reached the hospital I followed my father through the corridors. As we reached my mother's ward he said, 'There she is.' I followed his pointing finger and saw a shaven-headed woman. She looked so unlike the mum I had known all my life that I felt sick. As we went up to her bed she smiled but I don't think she recognized us. She had lost her power of speech, and her mind was not alert. She couldn't call out my name. It was several years before she could say it. Never again would she hold a conversation or remember anything that had happened. From that day on she wasn't my mum any more. She herself must have grieved because her eyes were often very, very sad. My brother next below me was about to marry but my mother couldn't do anything about preparing for it, as we had expected. My youngest brother was at university.

Within weeks the hospital sent her home. Within months physiotherapy was stopped. I stayed to look after her for six weeks. Quite suddenly one day she started to walk again but she could never use her left hand. Now and then she would say a word but that was all. Mostly she just sat smiling silently. She was a prisoner in her own body. The whole family was in a state of shock. Eventually I had to return home. My father and brothers felt helpless. They didn't know how to look after my mum. We didn't have any relatives in Britain. My grandparents in India were too busy looking after our land to come over.

I felt so frightened by this sudden turn of events. 'If this happened to me what would I do?' I thought. When I returned to Wolverhampton I grieved deeply for many months. As far as I was concerned my mother had died. Although I went to school I didn't speak to anyone. I didn't join in the laughter and jokes in the staff room as I used to . At home I continued to pray each evening, using the *gutka* as Sikhs do. We knew no other way of communicating with God. Just for the sake of peace, Sewa sat beside me. According to Sikh teaching, both men and women should cover their heads for prayer, so we used to put a piece of cloth on Sewa's head. I used a scarf. Poor Sewa, he couldn't even read Punjabi. He was distressed for me but didn't know how to comfort me. He and I were very close, closer than most Sikh couples Now, as I could no longer communicate with my mother, I came even closer to Sewa. Although we didn't say much to each other our actions showed our mutual love. Often I would pray, 'Send me someone who can teach me about you, God. I so much want to know you more.' In India I had been telling God what I wanted from him, but now I was asking him to reveal himself to me in his own way. I was expecting to meet a Sikh or Hindu holy man who could help me. I wouldn't go to the Sikh gurdwara because I thought, 'They don't know anything. I know more than they do because I've read more.' Anyway, women didn't ask spiritual questions in the gurdwara in those days.

However God didn't send a holy man. Instead one day in school he sent Celia who used to come and help me in the classroom. She would do whatever was needed: put out art materials for the children, help them with reading or dry the tears of one who was upset. She was probably in her fifties and had a lovely beaming smile. She used to comfort me too, like a mum. She was always talking about Jesus. One day she gave me a picture of Jesus Christ. She called it the sacred heart (she was a Roman Catholic). I took it and placed it on the wall in our house beside the pictures of the gurus. It made no difference to me whether it was the sacred heart of the gurus or of Jesus. I thought they were all ways to God. That picture really did help though, because I used to say, 'Look Jesus, I have prayed to all the gurus and all the deities but none of them has helped me. Will you help me please?'

About six months earlier the headmistress had invited the members of staff to come to church with her, on a special occasion, but we all said, 'No, thank you.' I said to myself, 'I'm a Sikh. Why should I go?' However, in assemblies, I started taking notice of what the headmistress said about God. I thought, 'How does she know so much about him?' I became more and more interested but I didn't say anything because the other teachers would have frowned on it. I didn't want them to know that I was interested in God because of the laughs they had about him in the staff room. But I used to think, 'If that's their Christianity, I never want to be a Christian.' Like most Asians I thought then that all westerners were Christians. Only the deputy head went to church. She was kind in her own way but I didn't really see the life of Christ in her.

The headmistress was a tall person, unmarried at the time, with her long, dark hair tied back. She had large brown eyes that always seemed to be smiling. She dressed modestly and carefully as befitted her position. One morning in assembly she talked about 2 Peter 3:8 ' With the Lord a day is like a thousand years, and a thousand years are like a day' (NIV). I have never forgotten that morning. The words penetrated deep into my heart. 'Is God really as great as all that?' I asked myself, 'If so what should I do about it?' Another day she talked about five missionaries who went by plane to a tribe in South America. Those primitive people killed them all. Later I learned that it happened in 1956 when Jim Elliot and four fellow missionaries went to the Auca tribe in South America. Her talks in assembly were now making a deep impression on my heart. She didn't know that someone sitting among the teachers was drinking it all in. I wanted to know more but I wouldn't ask her because I didn't want to appear to be currying favour with her. She was only about four years older than me but much wiser and more experienced. She was gentle and quiet in manner yet an excellent disciplinarian. She was never harsh with the children and would sometimes play with them. As far as the staff were concerned she was firm but pleasant. If you asked her advice she would give it but leave you to make the final decision.

My mind was still in a turmoil over my mother's illness. I continued to mourn over it and ask God, 'Why?' day in and day out. I didn't say anything at school. I just went sadly and quietly about my work. The other teachers could see I was unhappy but I couldn't bring myself to tell them why. Then one day, to my surprise, the headmistress came into my classroom, 'If I can help you in any way, come and talk to me,' she said. I pushed her away because I didn't want the other teachers to see that I was talking to her. Most of the staff didn't like her attitude and talked against her in the staff room. However, as I left school that day I couldn't get her out of my mind. Even during the night I continued to think about her mannerisms and her talks in assembly. So when school reassembled after the weekend she came to my classroom to greet me, as she normally did, and said, 'Hello. How are you?' I blurted out in return, 'Do you know something,? I'm searching for God. But there isn't anyone in our

Sikh temples who can tell me what I want to know. In your churches you have learned priests who can teach more about God. What do they have to say?'

She turned to me and said, 'I know you've got your own ways and your own religion but in church on Thursday evenings we women get together and learn from the Bible. Many questions are answered as we do so. You are free to come and join us if you would like to.' I was so desperate for answers that I said to her, 'All right. I'll come.' Then she left me. Later she came back and said, 'About coming to the meeting at church on Thursday. If Sewa will bring you, I will drive you home afterwards.'

When I reached home that day I said to Sewa, 'I want to go to church.' He had been brought up in Britain and was an agnostic but he said, 'All right. I'll take you.' So on Thursday evening we set out. When I walked into the church hall I saw there were twenty or thirty women, some already sitting in a semi-circle, others standing and chatting to each other. I didn't know what to expect. I just knew I wanted to hear what the others were saying and to be free to make up my own mind about whether I was receiving answers to my questions or not. Joan, my headmistress, was waiting for me and others said, 'Hello!' and welcomed me. There were no tactless enquiries about why I was there. I just felt a gentle sense of being received with love.

We sat down and Joan Thomas, the vicar's wife, led us in prayer and the singing of some hymns. She must have been in her fifties at the time, grey haired and of medium height. I have always loved singing, especially religious songs. As we sang something was happening inside me. My spirit was saying, 'I love it.' Then Joan Thomas read a passage from the Bible. Joan Salt, my headmistress, took out her own Bible and showed me where to find the passage. Then Joan Thomas spoke about what she had read. I listened to every word and each one went deep into my heart. Oh, how much I liked what she was saying. Afterwards we had a cup of tea and talked. Everyone seemed so loving. All my life I had longed to be with a group with whom I could feel at one because they loved God. I had never said to anyone that I did so. My mother had told me who God is and what he requires of us but nothing about personal love. In Sikh society we did not talk openly about such matters. But the ladies at the fellowship group did so that evening and I was thrilled.

Afterwards Joan Salt drove me back home as she had promised and I invited her in for a cup of tea. We sat talking for a while. I had lots of things on my heart but was not yet ready to share then all. She didn't pry or try to evangelize me; she simply befriended me. At school the next day she came and talked to me, again simply as a friend. From then on, every Thursday evening I travelled to church with Sewa and Joan brought me back. Gradually I felt safe to open up to her. She just listened and made a few appropriate comments, never trying to evangelize me or tell me I should turn to Jesus. Yet I saw the love and radiance of Christ in her. I will never forget her smile. I knew it wasn't the smile of an ordinary person but of someone who had a special relationship with God. She gave me some badly needed space while being fully available for me whenever I needed her. She was such a good listener as well as an encourager. I liked the way she called me 'lovie' sometimes.

Meanwhile my own spiritual and physical condition worsened. I agonized constantly over my mother's condition and grew extremely depressed. The doctor gave me some tranquillisers and sent me for tests at hospital. No one could find anything physically wrong with me, yet I continued to feel seriously ill. However I kept on attending the Thursday evening meetings and drinking in the truths I heard there. Little did I know that the whole church was praying for me. But God knew and responded. The time was not far away when I would experience deliverance.

8

Journey into Life

Joan continued to visit us on Thursday evenings. Our house had a through lounge so both Sewa and I were present when she came. We only gave her a cup of tea but she gave us much of her time.

On the very first evening I told her about my mother's illness. Then I explained how close I had been to her and how much I missed that closeness now. I did have Sewa alongside me but I needed another woman's comfort too. The very first night Sewa wanted to know about the church. I didn't even know what he was talking about. However because he had been brought up in Britain he had some understanding of church matters.

One evening later, I said to her. 'Family and social life in Indian society are so different from yours.' I questioned her about the differing role of women in our two societies. On another occasion we discussed the evils in both our societies — such as wife beating. Then we began to talk about God. I didn't tell her about my real feelings, especially not about how much I loved God. I didn't talk about my love for him to Joan or anyone else until I started giving my testimony. One night I talked about wanting God's holiness. Another time I spoke about what sort of character I expected of people who practised religion. We mentioned the differences between gurdwaras and churches. I complained about how horrid people can sometimes be. Another evening we talked about sickness and I explained how I struggled to understand it. Sometimes I asked how Christians discovered what God wanted them to do. She told me about the ten commandments. She always answered me quietly but firmly. When she didn't know the answers to my questions she would say so. We covered so many topics; everything except my own deep spiritual feelings and emotional needs. I was too shy to let anyone else know about them until I experienced the baptism of the Holy Spirit. Then one evening, after she had been listening to me, Joan said, 'You're talking like a Christian but you're not a Christian. Many of the matters you're talking about, like holiness, good conduct, respect for each other and so on, we Christians talk about too.' Later I realized that Sikhism's basic teachings are very similar to Christian ones.

Despite all our discussions I didn't understand what Jesus had done for me for months. Joan suggested I read John's gospel. I warmed to the idea but ended up reading Luke instead. At first it was just a story, like the stories I had enjoyed about the gurus from my childhood. Then I read the entire New Testament and found out something about Christian doctrine. I continued to attend Joan Thomas's Bible studies. As she talked I found God was talking to me. I still remember her teaching on prayer and the five fingers she held up to show us the different aspects of it: the index finger for God and those in full-time Christian work, the tall one for governments, the ring finger for family life, the little finger for the weak, poor and the sick, and the thumb for oneself. It was November when I first attended that Bible study and soon people were talking about Christmas, Carols by Candlelight and other celebrations of which I had never heard. I said to Joan Thomas, 'I can't join in these events because I'm not a Christian.' This was a Sikh way of thinking. If you're a Sikh you can't join in the celebrations of other religious groups. Then I said timidly, 'But I love singing. Would it be all right if I joined the ladies in that?' 'Of course, dear,' she said, 'of course you can come alongside us and join in.'

I loved being in the church because it was God's house and people talked freely about God there. After I came home from the first meeting, Sewa asked me what it was like and I said, 'Sewa, I want to go back. I feel they are people like me. I don't feel ashamed to say I love God because they all seem to do so.' I hadn't known people who talked about loving God before. If I told a Sikh I loved God, he or she would think I was a morally bad girl. In Sikh culture you don't say you love anybody else.

In those days I was involved in a deep inner struggle. I knew all about the Sikh Gurus, Baba Balak Nath and other deities but worshipping them wasn't satisfying me. About a year before, I had asked Sewa to bring me a copy of the Qu'ran from the library. However it didn't interest me, so we returned it. The Jehovah's Witnesses had also visited us. After talking to them I realized that their way of thinking was similar to Sikhism. They teach that you will only receive salvation through doing good works. I told them, 'Your teaching is the same as Sikhism. Please don't come back because I'm looking for something more.' I was really wanting something that would give me salvation without my having to do anything about it.

Just after Christmas, Joan Salt gave me a copy of a booklet called *Journey into Life*. I didn't read it straight away. When I did it didn't make sense, not for a long time. Yet I used the prayer at the end, without realizing that it was a prayer of commitment to Jesus. I just prayed it because I thought Jesus would help me if I did so.

Soon after that I stopped reciting the Sikh scriptures. However I would sit in front of the pictures of the Gurus with that of Jesus alongside. I sat cross-legged as Sikhs always do for prayer and asked Jesus questions about my mother's illness such as, 'Why did it happen?' Sometimes I just sat before him with a sad heart asking quietly, 'What's going on?'

I persisted in my efforts to find salvation. Joan Salt, Joan Thomas and others in St Jude's church were praying for me, though I didn't know it. Then I began to experience tremendous pressure from the spirits. All the creatures I feared most came alive in my sleep. Hundreds of snakes, lizards and all sorts of creepy-crawlies would crowd around me. Lizards would be about to bite me or a snake would look down menacingly from a tree. Sometimes I felt I was running from one place to another all night to try and escape from them. I would run to somewhere I thought safer, but when I arrived I was terrified to find the horrible creatures there too. In the morning I woke up exhausted. Often my face was covered with the tears I had shed in my desperation. During the day I didn't want to eat anything. I became deeply depressed but the doctor didn't know what to do for me. One night I felt at the end of my tether and said to Jesus, 'I've tried all the gurus, all the spirits I've known about from India, I've looked through the Qu'ran but I'm not getting anywhere. Will you please help me and get me out of this situation?' And to God, 'Tell me what you want from me.'

After that I didn't pray for a few days but my condition continued to deteriorate. I had no peace, no sleep and no desire to do anything positive. I asked Joan Salt if she knew of a place where I could find peace. I wanted to leave home and everything else in my life and never return. One day I even took up a bottle of tablets thinking there was nothing to do but end my life. Thank God, the fear of hell prevented me from swallowing them. Sikhism teaches that if you commit suicide you go straight to hell, so I was afraid of dying and going through the 8.4 million rebirths about which that religion teaches. One evening I watched *The World Around Us* on television and it showed colonies of snakes and other frightening creatures. It brought back all the fears I had had in India when I used to ask to be saved from reincarnation. I felt terrified of going through repeated births and rebirths, not always as a human being. One evening, when Sewa was out, I sat alone in the lounge terrified out of my wits. I screamed out to God, 'Give me salvation. I don't want to go through all those lives. I don't want to be a snake or some other horrible creature.'

All the time this was going on I continued going to church and reading my Bible. Yet God didn't seem to be listening to me. But one April night after we had gone to bed, and Sewa had fallen asleep, I thought, 'I'm going to read that prayer out of *Journey into Life* and I'm going to mean it. Let's see what Jesus will do then.' Before this I had prayed the prayer only understanding that I was asking Jesus for help. Now I determined to be a Christian whether my circumstances changed or not. 'Jesus I will belong to you whether you give me peace or not,' I said. Before that night I used to say, 'You make my mum better. You do this for me. You do that for me. Then I will be a Christian for you.' To bargain with God like this is a very Punjabi thing to do. We would say, 'If you answer my prayers I will send this much money here and that much money there, to holy places.' Tonight I would bargain no more. I would just come to Jesus and that would be all. So I rose from my bed, knelt by its side and prayed the prayer at the end of the booklet:

When Love Prevails

Lord Jesus Christ,
I know I have sinned in my thoughts, words and actions.
There are so many good things I have not done.
There are so many sinful things I have done.
I am sorry for my sins and turn from everything I know to be wrong.
You gave your life upon the cross for me.
Gratefully I give my life back to you.
Now I ask you to come into my life.

Come in as my Saviour to cleanse me.
Come in as my Lord to control me.
Come in as my Friend to be with me.
And I will serve you all the remaining years of my life in complete
    obedience.
Amen.

I meant every word and afterwards I said, 'I will be a Christian whether it changes anything or not. But you know I'm in urgent need of peace in my heart so, please Jesus, I beg you to do something about it.'

In the booklet it said that when you had prayed that prayer and become a Christian you should tell one other person, so I woke Sewa about 1 a.m. and said, 'I've become a Christian'. I didn't want to leave it till morning in case I changed my mind. All he said was, 'Oh, that's nice,' and went to sleep again. I settled down in bed and had a good sleep without nightmares.

When I went to school the next morning I didn't say anything to anybody because I didn't think my circumstances would change. After all they hadn't changed after the many times I had prayed before. However, three or four days later, as I sat in my classroom, I realized I had had no nightmares since the night I had committed my life to Jesus. For the first time in many weeks I felt hungry and wanted to live. My anger and frustration had disappeared too. Then I realized that Jesus had answered my prayer and done for me what he promised. I still didn't tell anyone except Sewa, even when I went to the Thursday Bible study.

One person I often talked to on Thursday evenings was Uncle Charlie. I used the name Uncle Charlie as a term of affection, because I had a special regard for him. He was an older man, with grey, receding hair. He worked in industry where it must have been tough being a Christian. He was straightforward and direct, always calling a spade a spade. After the Bible study he would tell me about the most basic matters of the Christian faith. I particularly remember him talking about God's love and justice and why Jesus had come. One evening people were discussing baptism and I asked him, 'How does one get baptized?' He replied, 'Why do you want to know? You're not a Christian.' 'I am', I said, and Joan, who was listening in, added, 'Yes, of course she is a Christian.' I hadn't told her I had made a commitment but she had seen the change in me. Then everyone gathered round and Uncle Charlie told them what had happened. I was amazed that they were all so excited. In the culture I came from you didn't talk about such personal things. I hadn't understood that telling others I had become a Christian would give them such joy. I thought of it as a personal matter between me and God. Also I was shy and had never opened up and talked about my most fervent spiritual desires. I was not sure whether I should tell them about the depth of my love for God because in Asian circles one does not talk about such things, especially if you are a woman.

However, even though I had made a commitment, salvation hadn't really gone deep into my heart yet. I had done it because I wanted Jesus to give me peace. That had changed me. Joan said she knew the day after I had prayed the prayer because the Spirit revealed it to her. But she didn't talk to me about it. She waited until I was ready to make an open confession. I thank God for her sensitivity.

Uncle Charlie continued to give me a lot of love. He is retired and probably about eighty now. After my declaration of faith in Jesus he talked to me on many evenings. He would tell me the little truths that a person growing up in a Christian atmosphere would have absorbed naturally, but of which I was quite ignorant. Especially I remember him helping me to understand why Jesus died for me. Yet, even so, it didn't go deep into my heart. The teaching of the Sikh gurus was still embedded there. It was hard for me to reorient my thinking in line with the new teaching I was receiving.

One Thursday, a few weeks after my conversion I said to
Sewa, 'I don't want to go to the Bible study. I'm on my own.' I
used to see all the English people around me and just one West
Indian lady, Mrs Murray. I longed to meet some Asians there.
All he said was, 'You go. You don't complain about being the
only Asian teacher at school.' One evening I told Joan Salt how
I felt but all she said was, 'Mrs Murray is there.' I loved Joan but
that remark made me realize how little most English Christians
understand the feelings of those of other races. A West Indian
was just as much a foreigner to me as an English person.

Something that upsets Asian Christians a great deal is the
tendency of English people to lump Asians and Afro-Caribbeans together. I have heard the term 'Black Anglicans' used
from the pulpit. This annoys an Asian, especially a new convert,
and is a bad witness to the latter. He says to himself, 'Who is
this man who is supposed to be working with us and doesn't
know the difference between Asians and Afro-Caribbeans?'
Sensitivity is needed in such areas. Anyone who works in a
mixed community needs to be aware of the issues which are
important to each group.

Thankfully my feelings of isolation soon passed. Even
though my English friends at church didn't understand all
about my struggles and problems, they did love me. It showed
in their words and actions. I began to feel 'adopted' by them.

9

Sewa's Journey

One couple in particular took me to their hearts. Mr and Mrs Thomas, the vicar and his wife. They were in their late fifties but still full of vitality. Mr Thomas was not very tall. By the time we knew him his hair was grey. Both he and his wife wore spectacles. He was humble and gentle but when he was preaching his voice rang out over the whole church. He didn't need a microphone. I always appreciated his teaching. He enjoyed studying languages and became interested in learning Punjabi. He used to pick up words and phrases from us and ask us what they meant. I remember him as enthusiastic, encouraging and loving. Both he and his wife are keen evangelists. They always welcome the stranger.

Mrs Thomas always dressed smartly. One day in her husband's study I saw a photograph of her when she was younger. It was beautiful so I said to him, 'Look at that gorgeous girl there. Now I know why you married her.' Mrs Thomas was sensitive, loving and caring. She was also an encourager. She never indulged in woolly conversation. All she said was to the point. She seemed to understand the difficulties I went through, and was always there for me when I needed her. She would never rebuff me with, 'No, I haven't got time.' Often she would put her arms round me and hug me so that I felt part of a caring family.

Mr and Mrs Thomas told me later that they realized that, although I had committed my life to Christ, I needed a great deal of support. They decided they would be that support. They promised God, 'We will be alongside Narindar as long as we are around.' They have kept that promise up to this day. Once I had become a Christian they began to pray for Sewa. Mrs Thomas told me later that she had persistently claimed Sewa for the Lord. And a Tuesday afternoon women's group that used to meet at the Thomases home prayed regularly for Sewa's conversion.

I used to go home from the Thursday Bible studies and tell Sewa what I had learned but he would take no notice. Joan continued to visit us. When she didn't know how to answer the questions I kept on asking, she would go and ask the Thomases. As I read the Bible on my own it began to make more sense but I still couldn't accept the teaching that I had to come to God through Jesus. After all I had been praying direct to God as Father for years. Jesus had given me peace, for sure. But why had he done it and not the ten gurus? I was sure the idea that one could only come to God through Jesus would annoy Sewa too.

Nevertheless I felt it was urgent that he should accept Christ. I would come home on a Thursday evening and tell him very plainly that he was going to hell, whereas I was not because I had turned to Jesus. When Joan and I talked, Sewa, who stayed in the sitting room with us, listened. Once, a few years earlier, when I had been ill, he had brought me a Bible, hoping it might comfort me. Now, unknown to me, he started to read it himself. Soon he had read the whole Bible without telling anyone.

At that time his kidneys were not working properly and he was waiting to go into hospital in Stoke-on-Trent for tests. He had had to do so on two earlier occasions also. I was scared of hospitals and would never visit him then. However this time when he was admitted Joan asked me if I would like to go and see him. I wasn't sure. Nevertheless she named a time when she would be at my house with her car. 'Then,' she said, 'if you want to go we will.' With her encouragement I felt I could face it. When we arrived, he was thrilled. A broad smile spread over his whole face and he said, 'The Lord has done a miracle. I have committed my life to Christ!' He told us that his blood pressure had gone so high that the medical staff were afraid he would die when they carried out the tests. When he came through safely he began to think, 'Where would I have been if I had died?' He remembered all he had read in the Bible and had heard Joan and me discussing and there and then accepted Jesus as his Saviour.

Joan and I travelled back to Wolverhampton with such joy in our hearts. It was late when we arrived but Joan insisted we go round and tell the Thomases. I said, 'But we don't want to make a nuisance of ourselves so late at night.' In the culture from which I came one didn't disturb priests unnecessarily. She replied, 'No, we must tell them right away.' When we arrived at the vicarage with our news Mr and Mrs Thomas were delighted. Mr Thomas sat with us and prayed for Sewa before we left. I was more thrilled than I had ever been in my life. Now there were two of us!

Later Sewa told me he had wanted to become a Christian for some time but he held back because he knew that our families and Sikh friends would turn against us. I was in such desperate need that that didn't bother me but Sewa thinks matters through carefully and counts the cost before acting. Even to this day he sometimes says to me, 'You still go on going into places where angels fear to tread!' Sewa is always there watching me. Even now he loves me to go ahead and take the initiative in any matter. However when he sees events starting to go wrong he comes to rescue me. That's the kind of rock God made him. Whereas I go emotionally up and down, he holds firmly to a decision once he has made it.

Joan continued visiting us on Thursday evenings and, even in school hours, I could count on her to help me if I got into difficulties. I talked to her about anything and everything, even about such problems as my relationship with my mother-in-law and other matters of Asian culture. Above all, though I was very independent, I needed support in learning the basic truths of Christianity. I still couldn't understand why I could only come to God through Jesus.

Then one day Joan said, 'Now you are Christians, you should be going to church on Sundays.' Slowly friends in the church realized that the family service would be the best one for us to attend. It would be easier for us to follow than the traditional morning and evening prayer. Once I had been, I wanted to continue, so Sewa and I started to go together.

At the same time my search for 'Why Jesus?' continued. I began to pray all hours of the day and night, 'Why must it be Jesus? How can he be the Son of God? Why can't I put him alongside the Sikh gurus?' I had read the truth in the Bible, I had heard it at church but it still hadn't sunk into the depths of my heart. I still wouldn't pray to Jesus although he was the one who

had healed me of the nightmares and given me peace. I continued to puzzle about the matter. Till one night, suddenly, a sort
of electric shock pierced my heart. 'It's true! He is the Son of
God!' I can't explain how or why it happened. I just knew it was
the truth. I was so certain that no one could change this understanding. It had gripped my heart so firmly. My faith deepened
significantly as a result. I had received much prayer and teaching but above all the revolution in my heart was the work of the
Holy Spirit. Nobody could have taught me to believe that Jesus
is the Son of God; the conviction had to come from him.

Even then I didn't realize that I had received salvation,
though I had heard about it repeatedly in church. It was months,
perhaps even a year afterwards, that I realized, 'Oh, I have
salvation too. I'm out of the 8.4 million rebirths cycle.' I was over
the moon with delight. Western Christians need to emphasize
this when talking to Hindu and Sikh enquirers. The idea of
reincarnation is so firmly embedded in their minds that it takes
a miracle of the Holy Spirit to remove it. Other faiths can give a
person religion. No one but the Holy Spirit can give them
salvation.

Within a few days, events began to happen in school as well.
One of the staff planned to take an assembly on Sikhism, but
Joan forbade it. The teacher concerned was extremely angry so
she turned to me for sympathy. 'Fancy stopping me doing an
assembly on Sikhism. Who does she think she is? 'she cried.
'After all you're not a Christian, are you?' I felt so scared. I hadn't
told anyone in school about the change in my life. However, in
the Bible studies on Thursday evenings, Mrs Thomas had told
us that we should never deny Jesus. Her words came forcefully
to my mind and I feared that if I denied him now he would deny
me on Judgement day. The Holy Spirit had put me on the spot.
So I answered gently, slowly and hesitantly, 'I am.' The look of
astonishment that crossed her face was plain to see. 'But I
thought you were a Sikh', she said. 'Yes, I was,' I replied, 'but
not any more.'

She was amazed and asked me many, many questions. Then
the other teachers gathered round also asking questions: Why
was I a Christian? When did I become a Christian? How? I told
them, 'Jesus has given me peace.' 'But surely your own gurus

could have done that', one of them commented.

'No,' said I, 'I've been asking them for a long time but they didn't give it. I've found answers in Jesus that I never found in Sikhism.' The teachers continued to put across the idea that the Sikh gurus are as good as Jesus but I said, 'They're not. Jesus is different. He has done things for me which they never did.' I think some of the staff were actually a little jealous of my experience of God, but they weren't prepared to say that Jesus is the only way to him.

They also started to notice changes in my behaviour. Previously I had joined in the gossip that went on in the staff room during every break in lessons. The teachers would talk about whoever was not present. Now I felt I couldn't join in that sort of conversation. The desire to be a holy person had been in my blood since childhood in India. I wanted to do nothing wrong. I don't know why. Perhaps because it was the only way I had known, in my youth, of achieving salvation. I had believed that the holier I became, the more chances I had of evading the cycle of reincarnations. So the change in my life after I accepted Jesus gave me the hope that I would now be able to achieve the holiness I had always desired. No spirit, no guru, no holy book had met my need, only Jesus.

The change in me continued to be a point of gossip in the staff room. Not only did the teachers ask me questions, they began asking Joan as well. Because of their interest, Joan arranged a meeting for all the staff at the Thomas' home. Margaret, a missionary from Japan, showed slides and talked. Afterwards one or two of the teachers commented, 'We are not Christians.' Sadly, no one else committed themselves to Christ despite their admission that they didn't know him as we did.

In the same summer the Don Summers Evangelistic Campaign took place in West Park, in Wolverhampton. Sewa and I attended every single evening. I took in the teaching like drinking glasses of water. With all my heart I sang,

Out of my bondage, sorrow and night,
Jesus I come, Jesus I come!
Into thy freedom, gladness and light,
Jesus, I come to thee!

I wanted to know more and more about God. One day, after a church service, Mr Thomas came and sat beside me and said gently, 'Narindar, you've been coming to church for some time now. Do you think you should be baptized?' As I still didn't know much about Christian practice, I said, 'If you think we should be, we will.' The next Sunday when we came to church he asked us about it again and said, 'Could you spare one evening for Bible study, in preparation?' We were delighted with this suggestion. So he gave us six months intensive Bible study. He based his teaching on a book called, *What would Jesus do?* I found it so stimulating that I based my life on it. One other phrase in the Bible particularly caught my attention, 'I am the Alpha and the Omega' (Revelation 1:8 NIV). This is mentioned in the Sikh Scriptures but Sikhs don't understand it. Only Christians realize that God is the source and goal of all of life. Mr Thomas went right through the Bible with us. He prepared the studies himself so that they met our individual needs. I don't know if he realized I was putting into practice every little detail he taught us. In those six months, my thirst for God increased even more. During the study time I often wept, crying, 'There is much more to God than you're telling me. How will I learn more?' I wanted to know all I possibly could. I used to pressurize every preacher I met and anybody else whom I thought knew more about God than me, 'You know more. You have to to tell me more. How do I go about learning it?' They did their best to teach me. Now I realize that I was going about it in the wrong way. Nobody can teach you the depths of God. You only experience them through your own walk with him. Mr Thomas gave me lessons in New Testament Greek as well. I love languages and only stopped learning Greek when I became too involved in witnessing. A burning desire to witness with boldness set fire to my heart. I talked about Jesus to everyone I met; old people, young people, small children. Nobody got away from me without hearing the gospel.

Late in 1979 Sewa and I were baptized. The day before the ceremony the spirits attacked me violently. Baptism is such a definite step. Not only does it mark you out as a follower of Jesus, it also demonstrates your break with your previous faith. The spirits were angry and determined to stop me going ahead if they could. The spiritual pressure they exerted was frightening. I prayed urgently to Jesus for protection and determined to go forward whatever the cost.

We were the first Asians ever to be baptized at St Jude's. One of our problems had been whom to ask to be godparents. Eventually, Mr Thomas suggested that the whole of the Thursday night Fellowship should act in that capacity. They are our prayer supporters even to this day.

We had already started attending the Wednesday evening prayer meeting at St Jude's. After our baptism we decided to attend all three services on Sunday, so that we could learn more. On Sunday morning I would wake Sewa and say, 'Come on, we want to go to Communion.' It was four miles to St Jude's from Sedgley and we would come home after Communion and go again for the 11 a.m. service. In the evening we would attend the 6.30 p.m. service. At those services I began to sense the same aroma that I had smelt on the roof of my village home in India years before; the aroma of *prasad*. Then I knew for certain that we were in the presence of God.

The church members simply adopted us. Almost every Sunday one family or another would invite us for lunch. Joan was the first to do so and others followed. We felt that we had become members of a large family. After the evening service we would have tea at the vicarage. I would sit by Mr Thomas, always asking questions and learning from him. He was only too ready to teach me. Everybody seemed to love us.

10

Becoming Aware of a Need

I continued to be hungry to learn more about God so I started reading my Bible in school whenever I had time to spare. Rather than joining in the gossip in the staffroom, I would sit in my classroom at playtime and lunchtime and pray and read. Once I read about Paul and how bold he was in witnessing for God, so I asked the Lord to make me like that. By now I was convinced that Jesus is unique and I wanted to go and tell everyone about him. To my joy he did give me opportunities to share the truth with nearly everyone I met.

About half of the children in my class were English, 25 per cent Afro-Caribbean and 25 per cent Asian. Their mothers were always friendly but now relationships with some of them began to take a new turn. Mothers began to come into the classroom and tell me their difficulties. One day an Asian woman came to the classroom when I was teaching and said, 'I want to talk to you. Will you come into the corner?' I did so and she said, 'My husband is beating me every day because he is having a sexual relationship with my older sister-in-law. I don't know what to do. Do you know how I could get help?' She couldn't speak English so I talked to Joan and she managed to arrange for a Punjabi-speaking social worker to see the woman. The following day she returned. Her husband had beaten her again and cut her hand with a knife. I think the social services took her away from her home for awhile. Later she returned home. But before long she left again. The saga continued for many years. Then I lost touch with her because her in-laws took her back to her husband's family in India.

Another woman used to try to talk to me at the classroom door. One day I said, 'Come after school. We can talk then without being disturbed.' She came at 3.30 p.m. At 5.30 p.m., when Sewa came to fetch me home, I was still telling her about the peace Jesus can give. After that many women, both Asian and English, came to open their hearts to me. They came to me at playtime, at dinner time and after school. I never talked to them when I should have been teaching. That would have been wrong. They would tell me about their difficulties and I would give them what practical advice I could. Then I would say, 'I know who can help you. Jesus gave me peace. He can give it to you as well. He can change your husband.'

If no one came for help I would spend my time reading the Bible and praying. I think it was because I prayed that God would use me that women came for help. The seeds of compassion sown in my heart at the age of fifteen started sprouting again. I have never been the sort of person to just stand and watch when someone is suffering. I must do something. Sometimes I think now I did too much. But when women were screaming with unhappiness, my immediate thought was, 'If only I could take their suffering away. I must do something to help them.' Some days I would go home to Sewa and say, 'I want to bring such and such a woman home. She's hurting.' Then he would say, 'No, you can't. Their husbands will come after you. What will you do then?' I think I was partly motivated by guilt. My life had been so comfortable. I had experienced so little of what these women were going through.

I spent one night crying because I had seen a woman in school whose husband had burnt the family's beds and beaten her up. He wouldn't give her any money for the child's dinner and she came to school to explain this. I saw some children coming to school on cold days with broken shoes because their fathers had spent all their money on alcohol.

All this brought back to my memory the years of growing up in India. Then I had seen how hard the women worked in the fields and how often they were badly treated. Sometimes they were beaten, sworn at and subjected to all sorts of ill-treatment. This had grieved me deeply. Now I was coming face-to-face with the same problem in Britain and had the opportunity to do something about it. I was learning a lot about the Lord's compassion. All the things I learned at church I determined to be obedient to in my heart.

However something was still lacking in my attitude. Some Asian prostitutes lived in Wolverhampton and I shrank from

dealing with them or teaching their children. The moral values
of India were still there in my soul and needed to be rooted out.

In some respects I made mistakes. My mother used to say,
'You don't know the world out there. People are often very
wicked.' I wouldn't take any notice then but now, through
experience, I have discovered that some cases are not genuine.
Some women exaggerate their problems or even make up stories in order to get your sympathy and gain a hold over you.
Maybe they sit in their homes longing for companionship and
see you as the answer to their isolation. Maybe they are jealous
of your friendships with other women. They want you to be
their friend rather than anyone else's. They want to possess you.
Some are greedy for what they feel you have that they don't.
Sometimes women said they had no money. Then, after I had
given them some, I found out they were taking a trip to India. I
don't know why the Lord chose me to serve him like this
because I was extremely green.

Now the desire to serve him that I had had in my teens began
to come back. I used to pray, 'I want to serve you, Lord. Let me
serve you.' I didn't even know what service to God meant, yet
day and night this prayer was on my lips. I used to say, 'You've
done so much for me. You've given me peace. Let me do
something for you.' My heart was constantly full of gratitude.
Now looking back I feel I had achieved the closeness to God that
I had always wanted. What a treasure the experience is! As a
child I had hoped to see God. Now I thought, I will be able to
see him because Jesus can do all things. He will make it possible.
I didn't want material goods; I didn't want power or position, I
only wanted God.

At that time I thought school was the only place of serving
God. I couldn't see anything beyond it. Sewa was a quiet and
steady person, going to work and coming home and listening to
me. Soon I started to say to him, 'This or that woman is having
a terrible time. Will you please take me to visit her?' So we
started visiting quietly. Nobody told us to do so. Nobody even
knew. We just saw the need and tried to help meet it. The
Thomases didn't know. Joan didn't know. I didn't have to tell
the staff at school because I was doing it in my own time.
Gradually I plucked up the courage to say, 'Jesus Christ can help

you.' I didn't know much about my new-found faith, but I did know that he could help them because he had helped me. So I began evangelizing within months of my conversion. I didn't know I was doing so. The word evangelism had not come into my vocabulary because in Sikhism there is no such expression. Looking back now I see I became an evangelist as soon as I became a Christian. It was the work of the Holy Spirit.

At night I would lie on my bed and think, 'When I go to visit this woman tomorrow, how can I help her?' Then something I should say or do would come to mind. Afterwards I would realize, 'These are not my thoughts.' I soon understood that they came from Jesus through the Holy Spirit.

Life had been going on in this way for some time when I received shattering news. Joan Salt was leaving our school to be a headmistress elsewhere. I never thought she would leave so soon. I had never trusted people easily but I had begun to trust Joan. She was the only person I could tell about my thoughts and feelings. I was a new Christian and every single day I needed clarification of what I read in the Bible and other Christian books. I needed much more help than even a secular westerner because I came from such a different background. Joan was the only one whom I felt I could ask about what I read and thought. I relied on her for my day-to-day fellowship too. When she left I missed her terribly and cried a great deal. She phoned me every day to see if I was all right. Then gradually I found my feet without her. Later she married and Sewa and I went to college so we drifted slowly apart. Now I think what happened was God's way of separating us. I had become too dependent on her. I was like a child whom the mother wants to stop feeding. Sometimes she has to make him do without the breast to force him to feed himself. Similarly God wanted me to look after myself, drawing all I needed from him. I didn't feel ready for that but he forced me to be. I had no one but him on whom to depend now.

I didn't find it easy in school after Joan left. She and I had tried to be discreet about our friendship. Nevertheless the staff did know that we were both Christians and would support each other. Now she had gone, I faced subtle opposition in many ways. When I walked into the staffroom everything would go quiet. I knew there was opposition but I couldn't put my finger on it, so I couldn't say anything to them. I did say to one of the more friendly teachers, 'This is getting too much.' She herself didn't want to come to the Lord but she said, 'Go on with what you've found. Don't let anyone stop you.' The opposition made me feel quite lonely, but I had taken a decisive step in committing my life to Jesus and I meant to pursue it at all costs.

11

Costly Discipleship

When I found myself facing opposition from the staff I comforted myself with the thought that at least my father would understand. The Christmas before my conversion he and my mother and brothers had come to visit us and I had told him I was going to church. 'I'm in search of God and the Sikh scriptures don't satisfy me any more. At the Christian church I'm learning what I want to know.' He encouraged me to keep on going, saying, 'I went to church once and the preaching impressed me.'

A week or two after I had become a Christian we went to tell him. I expected that he would be pleased, but instead he was so angry he nearly threw me out of the house. 'Why do you have to leave the Sikh God and go and accept the Christian one? It's all the same,' he shouted. 'You're letting down the family. 'What is so different about this God?' 'I spent a lot of money on your education and now you do this to us!' He also said many things that didn't make sense because he was angry. He didn't speak to us for the rest of the time we were there.

I felt extremely upset. My mother was still ill and unable to understand what was happening, so I couldn't explain to her. That grieved me. In addition, a dreadful fear came over me. Suppose what had happened to her should happen to me one day. What would I do? This fear gave me more incentive than ever to search for God. I was sure that only he could help me if ever it did happen. I thought, 'My mother had all us children to help her. Sewa and I have no one. Who would look after me in such a case?'

We returned to Wolverhampton the next day. Frequently I found myself weeping. I had lost my mother and now it seemed I had lost my father too. On hearing what had happened, Mr Thomas came to see me. He sat by my side for quite a long time while I wept and wept, but still I didn't feel comforted. Many days passed before I felt God's love coming directly into my heart to comfort me.

My father didn't speak to me for years after that. Sometimes I would visit the family when my sister-in-law had a baby. I would say to my father, 'Hello, papa-ji.'[1] He would say, 'Hello,' and then turn away. He wouldn't speak to me again for the rest of my visit. As time went by, I began to realize more of how my father and two brothers felt about my conversion. They were lonely and upset after my mother's illness, and my turning to Christ made them feel I had rejected them. I deserted the family just when we needed a sense of being one in our troubles. I had not given them or my mother the care they expected. They just didn't know how to handle all their conflicting emotions. They wanted me to be there for them just as they were there for me. They were deeply shocked and found my action difficult to understand or even tolerate. As for me I had chosen the path of following Christ and I meant to keep to it though it broke my heart. I was convinced of the truth of Acts 4:12: 'Salvation is found in no one-else, for there is no other name under heaven given to men by which we must be saved' (NIV).

After Sewa's conversion, his family was shocked too. They went cold at first, then angry. They commented on all our new behaviour. Sewa's parents did actually attend our baptism, even though they weren't happy about it. When a Sikh girl marries, her brother should escort her in a walk round the holy book. At Sewa's sister's marriage he refused to do this and it caused a lot of trouble between us and his family. They were always finding something about which to quarrel with us. One day an *akhand path* (a reading of the entire Guru Granth Sahib) was being held at the gurdwara and Sewa's mother came to church to get us to attend. She stood outside the church, tears rolling down her face saying, 'You tell me what you want us to do. Whatever you want, I will do for you. Why won't you come to the *akhand path*?' On another occasion she said to us, 'Do we have to make an appointment to see you now?' Soon after becoming Christians, we began to invite needy young women to stay with us for a while. Sewa's mother came to our house once and found two of

1. A term of respect used when addressing an older person or someone in a superior position to the speaker.

them there. She shouted at me, 'What are you doing with these girls? Don't have them in the house. They will do all sorts of bad things to you one day.'

Then we realized that if we kept up close relationships with our families they wouldn't let us serve God in the way we felt he wanted. So we made a decision. If we were to serve God then it must be 'No' to the family. This wasn't easy because although they were angry with us, they wanted us back. They kept phoning and asking us to come back but we stuck to our decision not to become entangled with them again.

The same thing happened with friends. I saw them in a new light and didn't like what I saw. Most of them were out to please themselves, to spend money on entertainments, meals out and plenty of new clothes. They had no concern for anyone except themselves. One day I fasted and prayed at home because I knew the time had come to let go of our old friends. We used to eat together, visit the cinema together and spend time together gossiping. I now knew these activities were taking me in the wrong direction. From that day I laid aside all old friendships. It was hard because friendships mean a lot to anyone. We became extremely lonely but chose to be alone in order to lead the sort of life we knew God wanted. It was an immense sacrifice but he strengthened us to keep to our resolution.

Breaking off ties with our families didn't mean we ceased to care for them. I started thinking about their salvation more and more. I prayed, 'Jesus, you have given me salvation. Please give it to my mum, to my family.' I spent hours praying for them, and even for relatives I had never met. I concentrated so much on praying, for my mother in particular, that I wasn't very attentive to the needs of others. However, one day I believe the Holy Spirit spoke to me, saying, 'Do you love your mother more than I do? I have made her.' That gave me fresh and deep understanding. From that time on I haven't grieved over my mother's illness or anything to do with the families. I felt so encouraged to realize how much God loved them. He could take care of them much better than I. After that revelation I concentrated on going out and about, visiting needy people and paying close attention to my job. I also spent more time with mature Christians who could teach me what I need to know about God.

12

The Holy Spirit

When I found Christ, I found a treasure. In my childhood and
teenage years I had wanted to be close to God. He had satisfied
my spiritual hunger to some extent then. Only when I became
a Christian did I realize that that was just preparing the soil of
my heart for the day when he would lead me to Jesus. Now that
desire to know him more closely had come alive again and gave
me no rest. I started praying, 'I want to know more,' because I
felt dissatisfied with what I was receiving. When I sat in church
I used to cry a lot, telling God, 'There's much more of you. Let
me know you'. Often I said to Christian friends, 'You know
more. You're not telling me about it. Why aren't you telling me?'
Whenever a Christian came to our house I would ask them
about the Lord. 'Tell me more, tell me more. What do you know
about Jesus? What do you know about God? I want holiness. I
want all that he is. I want to see him.' I was so stubborn about
wanting so much of God. Friends would say, 'You can't learn
everything overnight.' But I would answer, 'Why not? I want to
learn so quickly'.

Then I found another way. I developed a prayer life on the
same lines as I had in India. I spent days and nights in prayer. I
told him I never wanted to do anything wrong. I wanted absolute holiness. People told me it wasn't possible in this life but I
wasn't dissuaded. I continued a quiet search for many years. I
knew that Jesus had answered my prayer for peace as none of
the gurus had and that he was the one I had desired all my life.
The more I prayed, the more I loved him. Something in me was
continually full of joy and love for him.

One day I became intensely frustrated because I felt I was not
getting the closeness I desired. I wasn't talking to God face to
face as Moses and the prophets did. I was reading my Bible and
trying to base my life on those people whom I read about in the
Old Testament. I was willing to learn from anyone who would

give me my heart's desire to live close to God. Looking back now I think I was asking for supernatural power so that I could live in this world but not be like most people in it. The feelings, habits and attitudes I saw in others I knew were also part of me. I didn't like them. I wanted the whole of myself changed.

At one time I was reading the book of Job. At the end of it I felt he had found the answer to his desire for God. It seemed to me that he had a special relationship with God. I wanted that too. So one afternoon I sat and prayed to God, 'Lord if you will let me have the kind of relationship you had with Job after he suffered so much, I will suffer too.' I gave an open invitation to God. Within days I knew something had happened but I didn't relate it to the prayer I had prayed. Something inside me had changed. I often cried in church. Through my Bible college years I spent most of my nights crying. There was so much in me that wanted to see God; to have the closest possible relationship with him. When I tell anyone else about my prayer they seem to think I did wrong but I know I didn't. God allowed me to suffer because I had prayed for it. I had so much love in my heart that I was almost breaking with its power. I don't know whether anyone else has felt like this. I was willing to die for love of God. That's why I offered myself to suffer.

All my life I had felt a little guilty because I had never known suffering. As I talked to the women and girls who came to me at school, I felt even more so. They were broken-hearted, rejected, frustrated and often angry with society for letting them suffer. I felt I owed them something because I had escaped anything of that sort. I know it may sound strange, but somehow I feel more complete for having suffered. To some extent the prayer to know God more is still on my lips, but at the same time I'm scared, because learning to do so has meant a lot of pain.

One day a friend came to see me and I was moaning to her, 'You Christians aren't telling me more about God. You know more than me but you're not telling me.' So she started talking about the Holy Spirit. I had learned about him from the Bible studies with Mr Thomas. He had told us about the book, *Nine O'Clock in the Morning* and gone through a course with us where he mentioned a lot about the Holy Spirit. But I hadn't come to grips with the fact that he was the third person of the Trinity. He was a mystery to me as Jesus was at one time.

When my visitor mentioned the Holy Spirit I told her I wanted to learn more about him. Then she told me about some meetings that were to take place shortly at the Methodist church. Colin Urquhart would lead a three-day conference. 'Come with me for one session,' she said, 'if you don't like it, you don't have to come back again.' She told me afterwards that she really feared taking me. However she took a chance and God honoured it.

Sewa and I went to the first meeting and I loved every minute. I had never been so moved. I wanted more and more of what Colin Urquhart was teaching. I wrote down every word he spoke and, not for any known reason, wept and wept. When we arrived home I said to Sewa, 'I want to go again.' We went every day, to every session. Afterwards we went and told Mr and Mrs Thomas. They were encouraging.

Now I knew what more it was that I wanted. I wanted the fullness of the Holy Spirit so that I could live a holier life. I understood that he changes a person from within and I wanted my ways changed immediately. However this was not the Lord's will. He taught me slowly. I was impatient and felt he wasn't teaching me fast enough. So I spent a lot of time in prayer and fasting. Nobody told me about fasting. I just read about it in the Bible and thought I should do it. I didn't tell anyone, but I was fasting all hours of the day and night; just because I felt frustrated at not learning about God more quickly. I also read books by Dennis and Rita Bennett and others who wrote about the work of the Holy Spirit. I began to speak in tongues. Nevertheless I still wanted more. I began praying to be with people like myself whose one desire was to know the Lord more closely. 'Then,' I thought, 'I will learn more about the work of Jesus and the Holy Spirit.' I was also praying, 'Let me serve you God.' Every spare minute, even when I was on playground duty, I was saying those words in my heart.

One evening I went to an inter-church meeting. Across the room I saw Douglas Field, the Methodist minister in whose church Colin Urquhart had held the meetings I attended. Douglas is of average height and going a little bald. He doesn't have an impressive presence. He is gentle and unassuming but when he speaks he does so with quiet authority. Normally, I am shy in new surroundings, especially with people I consider senior to myself. I longed to speak to him but didn't want anyone to know about my spiritual feelings or my background. However, after the meeting, something just pushed me towards him. I went up to him and said, 'I want to know more of what Colin Urquhart talked about.' Douglas replied that he held a learning group in his house on Friday evenings that we were welcome to attend.

Sewa was not too keen to go but I was, so he said, 'All right, I'll take you and stay with you. We'll see how it goes this one time. Afterwards we can decide if we want to keep on going.' It had been a Thursday when I spoke to Douglas. I was burning with desire to experience his meetings so we went the very next day.

Douglas taught us about the work of the Holy Spirit in detail, often using tapes from Colin Urquhart. There were only a few of us but I found it a special group. We prayed a great deal too. One evening, as we were praying, I felt so tired I thought I was going to fall asleep. Suddenly, I saw myself getting up from my chair, yet leaving my body there. I followed a man who started walking in front of me. We walked for a while until we reached a large hall. We crossed it and came to a door. We went through it into a little corridor. It was dark, but after a few yards, when my eyes became accustomed to it, I saw that there were rooms on both sides. They were like dungeons with iron bars in place of doors. I could see at a glance that people were imprisoned behind them. I continued to follow the man. I wasn't afraid, though it seemed a very frightening place. On the left-hand side I saw small fires here and there at a distance. Smoke billowed out from them. It was a horrifying place but I kept on following the man, feeling full of confidence. I could hear the people moving about behind the bars. Suddenly, a woman put her arm through the bars in front of me. She was holding a silver bowl but it didn't obstruct my progress. I just kept on walking. She cried out, 'Help me! Help me!' The man knew I had softened and wanted to do something for her. Immediately he turned round and looked at me and I knew it was Jesus. He said, 'You can't help her now.' That was it. Immediately I was back in my body again. When we had finished praying I told the group what I had seen. Douglas said, 'The Lord is showing you the plight of those in hell.' That gave me even more zeal and enthusiasm. I wanted to help people here and now so that they would be saved from hell. Once they're dead it will be too late. That experience was another stepping stone in my call to be an evangelist.

At the same time as I was learning about the Holy Spirit and experiencing him at work in my life, I was also under attack from evil spirits. I told Douglas and Catherine and they came to our house several times. They always listened to what I had to tell them about my life with quiet attention and then they prayed with me. They are middle-aged now, both short and stocky, going grey and full of wisdom and love. Douglas is calm but Catherine is quite emotional. When you tell them with tears about some experience you have had, she is quite likely to cry along with you. Her guidance helped me tremendously. She spent many hours praying with me. Douglas is deeply sensitive to the needs of others. Together they loved me with God's love. I soon felt as though I had been adopted into their family. A deep sense of caring always came across to me as they prayed and commanded the evil spirits to leave. But despite their ministry I still didn't feel free. I seemed to be under some form of spiritual oppression. So they suggested I go away to a place where I could receive more concentrated help. Sewa and I went to a Wholeness Through Christ School of Prayer for five days. Each of us had two or three hours with a man and a woman counsellor while the rest prayed. There were thirty of us and the whole experience was like being in a powerhouse of prayer. Through the Holy Spirit the people ministering to us would see pictures related to our experiences. Sometimes we ourselves saw pictures or found ourselves catapulted back into frightening experiences from the past. When we told the two counsellors what we were seeing they prayed for our release from the grip of the evil spirits, and the healing of the hurts from the past. For me it was tremendously helpful. I was released from a number of binding spirits from my earlier life.

Sometimes I do still have a nightmare or a frightening time

when I am alone in the house. Catherine Field helped me over that. Once she said to me, 'Look, Narindar, learn to tell the evil spirits off when they frighten you. The Holy Spirit is your protector. If you command the attackers to leave you alone, in Jesus name, they will have to do so.'

Now I have been a Christian for fifteen or sixteen years, I realize that if the spirits have a hold on your life they don't let go easily. That's why those of us becoming Christians from other faiths should hold on tightly to the Lord Jesus Christ. Satan is very active and never pleased when one of those he has had in his clutches becomes a Christian. He will never let them go voluntarily, but will fight hard to keep them. He will only release his hold when someone experienced in confronting evil spirits commands them to go in Jesus' name. People who come out of other faiths have to be extremely careful in their walk with the Lord.

At Christmas 1980 I had my first experience of public ministry when I read John 1 to the congregation. Mr Thomas then interviewed me and I gave my testimony. I didn't really know what testimonies were, but Mr Thomas asked me questions and I gave answers. Afterwards, I felt great and God assured me that I had done the right thing. Sewa was reluctant to talk about his experience of God. In those days Sewa wouldn't talk much. He just let me get on with it.

Mr Thomas taught us basic Christian doctrine before our baptism, going right through the Bible from Genesis to Revelation. It was marvellous work but I was keen for more. We heard that a party from St Jude's was going to a Convention at Keswick, in the Lake District, in the summer. We would receive deeper teaching there. I was keen to join them and we did so in the following July.

When we arrived in Keswick I felt thrilled by the beauty of this small lakeside town. And when I saw the big tent where the meetings were held I was amazed. I had never seen one so large. Nor had I ever seen so many Christian bookstalls lining the street that led to the main tent. I don't know how many people crowded into it for meetings; perhaps five thousand. They were of all races and backgrounds, as the message over the doorway, 'All One In Christ Jesus', proclaimed.

I deeply appreciated Alec Motyer's Bible readings on the Psalms. When some people were saying, 'Alec Motyer! That was a bit too much for me,' I was loving it. I made notes of everything he said. I also bought the tapes of his talks. For a long time I wouldn't let go of them. I had to take them wherever I went. Sewa and I went to all the meetings. His spiritual hunger was not as great as mine and he used to drag his feet. But I made him come with me. I used to say, 'We are together whether you like it or not', and he came.

The fellowship we experienced with the rest of the party from St Jude's church was tremendous too. We lived together in the same guest house so we met each other constantly between meetings. We held animated conversations over the meal table. We went for walks together. We prayed together in the evenings. Everyone was so loving and looked after us so well. I saw so much godliness in that group. The whole experience was something I had never met in Sikh circles.

We also met an Asian Christian family. They had come from Pakistan and were working full time for the Lord in Sheffield. I had been longing to meet somebody from my own background. Although they were not from Sikhism, we became close friends afterwards. They came to visit us with their four daughters on more than one occasion and we had a lovely time together They had actually left Pakistan especially to come and serve God in Britain. How I admired the missionary spirit that had led them to do that.

The following January we were baptized and in the June we were confirmed. Again that summer we went to Keswick. Alan Redpath was one of those who preached. His words are with me to this day. I remember one illustration he gave. 'You say, as you go to bed, that you want to get up early in the morning to pray. You ask the Lord to wake you. He will do so, but you will have to get out from under the blanket yourself.' He also told us that when he was younger, he used to meet a friend to pray early in the morning. They lived by the sea. The first time he went to their meeting place on the beach he found his friend crying. He thought, 'That's really what praying is all about: pouring your whole heart out to God. Wet eyes, bent knees, broken heart are the most acceptable attitudes before the Lord.'

I have walked in that teaching ever since. The books Alan Redpath has written have also helped me, especially *Victorious Christian Living* on Joshua and *Victorious Christian Service* on Nehemiah.

At the missionary meeting, on the final day at Keswick, Alan Redpath preached on Isaiah 6:8 (NIV). 'Who will go for us?' His message stirred my heart. I was ready to go anywhere and do anything God wanted. Then the chairman of the meeting asked those who were willing to commit themselves to serve the Lord, wherever he might lead, to stand. We did so. The stewards gave us cards that confirmed what we had promised. I still have that card to remind me of my commitment. However Sewa had stood a little reluctantly and I knew he wasn't ready. So when we came home I kept on praying for God to light the flame in his heart that he had in mine.

13

Co-heirs and Co-workers

One morning a few months after my confirmation I heard God's voice in my heart, as I'm sure we all do at times. He said to me, 'I want you to have your marriage blessed.' I replied, 'All right, Lord, I'll tell Mr Thomas.' Then I thought, 'No, I'll tell Mrs Thomas.' I was still rather shy of talking to the vicar. I asked Sewa about it and he agreed, so I spoke to her. She said, 'Narindar, Alan and I were talking about you and Sewa a couple of days ago. We wondered if you would ever come to the point of having your marriage blessed. And now here you are!' The summer term was almost at an end. The Thursday Fellowship closed over the holidays so they said, 'We will have the blessing on the closing evening and make it a celebration.' Sewa and I replied, 'We would like to invite all the church and provide refreshments.' That's a very Asian way of doing things. Then I said to Mrs Thomas, 'Will you take control?' and laughingly, 'Just think, you haven't a daughter but, if you had, you would have made all the arrangements for her wedding, wouldn't you? So will you do it for me?'

What a wonderful experience the blessing was! I wore an orangey-yellow Punjabi suit and a blue sapphire ring. In India orange and blue are considered holy colours. When Sewa and I reached the church we saw that the men were all wearing their best suits and the women pretty dresses, as if it were a real wedding. Some of the ladies had also decorated the church with sprays of flowers. Our friends at St Jude's have given us so much love.

Mr Thomas put the service together specially for us and led it in a loving manner. It was a special experience for us though I have forgotten now what he said. I do remember that we had prayers and a Bible reading and appropriate wedding hymns. At one point we knelt together before him. He put our hands together and dedicated our marriage to the Lord. Then he gave us a card on which were written the words, 'We are co-heirs

with Christ'. At the time I didn't understand their meaning but
in recent years I have realized that all that is available to Jesus
is available to us. The crucial point is how we make use of it.
After the service everyone enjoyed the refreshments we had
provided and many of our friends congratulated us. I felt things
change that evening between Sewa and myself. Spiritually we
came closer than we ever had before. One evening a Methodist
minister came to our house for a meal. As we were eating he
said, with a laugh, 'The Lord wants to come into your marriage
now.' That's when I understood the full meaning of Christian
marriage. We had a Sikh wedding ceremony originally but the
Christian blessing of our marriage had much deeper signifi-
cance. It meant we were both fully dedicated to the Lord.

Many things began to happened after that. One morning in
church a voice spoke to me — an audible voice — not the one I
usually hear in my heart. There was one voice I specially loved
hearing on a certain television programme. It had depth and
sweetness. Only the Lord knew how much I liked it. Now it was
as if someone had turned on the radio because that same voice
said, 'All your prayers will be granted.' I knew it was the Lord's
voice. No one else heard it. I looked around but couldn't make
out where it came from. I didn't say anything to Sewa but as we
came out of church he said, 'I believe God spoke to you today.'
I looked at him and asked, 'How do you know?' He replied, 'I
just know. I just feel that he spoke to you.' That was the confirmation I needed because I had been confused and wondered if
I had imagined it all.

Another time when we were in a difficult situation, Sewa
said, 'You know, when it comes to the crunch, Narindar, your
faith in the Lord is so strong.' I tried to explain that it's nothing
to do with my faith. It's just the fact that I know God is with me
and one day he will sort out every problem. I never doubt that
he is present and listening to my prayers.

One evening at St Jude's, Mrs Thomas came up to me after
the service and said, 'Narindar, two Asian girls walked in
during the worship. Come and speak to them.' At that time I
was the only Asian woman in the church so only I could easily
relate to them. Mrs Thomas took me by the hand. I walked along
with her without having any idea what I was going to say. When

I saw them I felt overcome with love for them. I held their hands and hugged them. Then I started to talk to them in a way I had never done before. I felt as though someone else was talking through me. We became friends there and then. I invited them to our home. I felt they needed a great deal of love. I didn't witness to them in any special way or tell Bible stories as people may have thought I should. All I told them was that I was a Christian and loved the Lord Jesus. Otherwise I just cared for them and identified with their situations. Three or four years after our first meeting they became Christians. They have remained steadfast since. That first evening was an answer to my prayer, 'I want to serve you, God.' I didn't realize it at the time, but it was the beginning of our work for the Lord.

In those early days I would have loved to see members of St Jude's coming forward to help in the work amongst Asians and was disappointed when no one did. Now I realize that they didn't know how to work with people of a different culture. Some church members did ask me, 'Why don't you bring more like yourselves?' I said openly, 'You're not ready.' I wasn't afraid to say so because I felt a oneness in Christ with them. This had started at Keswick and grew and grew so that I was never afraid to speak plainly to them. Because Sewa and I are quite westernized, we had been able to adapt to their ways of doing things. Other Asians wouldn't find it so easy. Anyway, my remark made an impact. Some St Jude's members asked us to explain Asian ways to them. As a result, they began to welcome Asians to the church.

One summer in the early eighties we went to another Don Summers' Crusade in West Park in Wolverhampton. We attended every day and I felt myself being immersed in the teaching. One evening when we reached home Sewa told me an English person had approached him and spoken in Hindi. Sewa had never learned to read or write Hindi, never mind speak it. When this stranger realized that Sewa spoke fluent English they conversed in that language. His name was Mr Summers. A group of Asians was with him. He had been a missionary in India for many years and was using his experience there to help him relate to Asians in Britain. He said to Sewa, 'You should join our group. We do everything in Punjabi.' Sewa replied, 'We'll think about it.' We were hesitant about being involved with them because Sewa and I had run away from the Asian community when we moved to Sedgley to live among English people. Although I was drawing closer to Asian women as they came to me at school, we were still indifferent to Asians as a whole. I had become independent and didn't want to return to the old traditions, especially those concerning the position of women in society.

We didn't pursue that contact any further at the time. However I began to wonder, 'Are there any more Asian Christians in Wolverhampton? Is there a Bible in Punjabi?' I had seen Indian Christians in India, but my family had always kept me away from them. I started to think, 'I'm fluent in Punjabi. Perhaps I can write something for the Lord in that language.' Despite our rejection of the Asian community, I was longing to meet some other Punjabi Christians.

One Sunday a couple from Birmingham came to speak in St Jude's. Desmond Dansey had been a missionary in both Burma and India and Enid, his wife, in Africa. After their retirement to Britain they met and married. Now they were running a book shop in the Lozells area of Birmingham where they sold literature in Asian languages as well as English. That day Desmond spoke about India and then about relating to Asians in Britain. His message created a great desire in my heart to serve the Lord full-time. But how could we when Sewa wasn't ready? Afterwards Mr Thomas introduced us to them and Enid said, 'You will come to see us in Lozells, won't you?'

A few weeks later Alan Thomas preached on the same words we had heard at Keswick, 'Who will go for me?' Then and there I prayed, 'Lord I'm ready to go, but please send Sewa with me.' He and I were not seeing eye to eye. He was worried about how we would pay the bills if we went into full-time Christian service. I felt sure the Lord would provide for us.

One day Joan Salt said to me, 'Let's go and see the Danseys.' So one Saturday we went. Desmond was a tall man, gracious and tactful. His face radiated peace. He never boasted about anything he had done but spoke with humility. Enid was tall too and down-to-earth. You could always talk to her, knowing she was listening with sympathy. Lozells is a multi-racial area of Birmingham. Desmond and Enid's shop was one of a row of similar shops almost all owned by Asians. The Danseys lived above the shop so they were in frequent contact with these neighbours and on good terms with all of them. Desmond and Enid sold Christian leaflets and books in a variety of Asian languages including Hindi, Urdu, Punjabi, Bengali and others. They also sold literature in English as well as pencils, biros, rubbers and other materials for the children. At Christmas they sold Christian calendars and Christmas cards. They had a love for people that was evident to whoever came into the shop, adults, teenagers, children, black, English and brown. When Joan and I visited them, I saw how much they needed help, especially with the language. I longed to work with them but how could I without Sewa? I continued praying, 'Let me know you. Let me serve you. Let me come closer to you.' I wasn't asking for wealth or even health but just for opportunities for service.

Marlin Summers and his wife, whom Sewa had met at the Don Summers Crusade, kept on asking us if we would go to their services. However we were still running away from Asians. Nevertheless they asked us to give a home to a young Asian woman in their fellowship. Her family had turned her out because she had become a Christian. I mentioned Mr Summers' request to Mr Thomas. He said, 'Narindar, you have received so much teaching from God. Now a time has come when he wants you to serve him too. By receiving this girl, you are receiving the Lord Jesus Christ into your heart.'

So Nirmla came to us just before Christmas. She was a Punjabi Christian in her early twenties, a small girl with a fair complexion. She had a pleasant personality, so when she asked us to go with her to the Christmas celebrations at the Summers' Fellowship we agreed to do so. First of all we worshipped in Punjabi, singing Christmas songs and hearing the Christmas story. The children performed a nativity play. Afterwards we all sat down together for a curry meal. It was our first introduction to Asian Christians in Wolverhampton. I hesitated about approaching individuals. I feared the women would gossip about problems in the home; especially that mothers-in-law and daughters-in-law would grumble about each other. One or two people welcomed us and one or two put us off so I wouldn't go again. I determined to pursue holiness in my daily walk with the Lord Jesus and to obey him in everything. Gossip offended me. Later, Mr Summers phoned and asked if I would teach Sunday School at his Fellowship. I hesitated and he said, 'Pray about it.' However I still wasn't ready.

That Easter we went to Spring Harvest. One day we heard a message on Abraham. The speaker emphasized that Abraham left everything and went where God wanted him to. Amazingly, it made little sense to me but it meant a great deal to Sewa. After the meeting he said to me, 'God is calling us. We must leave everything and go.' This brought a revolution in Sewa's attitude towards serving.

After coming home we put our house up for sale in obedience to God. We wanted to be ready to go wherever he took us and do whatever he wanted. We put away our television and anything else we thought might distract us from our call. Sewa initiated it all. We worked five days a week at our secular jobs and then started going to Lozells on Saturdays to help Desmond and Enid Dansey. I went visiting with Enid. Sewa looked after the shop with Desmond. Desmond was a tactful person. He wouldn't confront you directly about any matter concerning you, so that you could keep your dignity. He would give an illustration of something and express his view about it. Then he left you to work out the implication for yourself. Enid was different, she sometimes became worked up over issues and you knew she was upset. I found this a help because it meant she understood my changes of mood too.

At the same time, Sewa began going to Marlin Summers' Bible study group in Punjabi on Friday evenings, while I continued to attend the meeting at the Fields' home. On Wednesdays, we went to the prayer meeting at St Jude's and I still went to the Ladies' Fellowship on Thursdays. On Sundays, we went to the 8 a.m. communion at St Jude's and back to the 11 a.m. service. In the evening, we went to the Summers' fellowship.

After a few months Nirmla left us to go to Bible college. We rejoiced that we had been able to play a part in the work God was doing in her life. However having her to stay gave us the idea of using our home for the Lord. I deeply desired to serve

God and started asking him and my teachers, such as the
Thomases and the Danseys, how I could do so. I hoped to go
overseas somewhere. Perhaps I could work in a Christian
school. The gift of teaching was the only one I knew I had.
However the Lord had different ideas. He took me into a ministry I wasn't keen on: using my home for him.

By nature I was shy and found it hard to speak to strangers.
At home in India, when we had visitors whom we didn't know,
my two brothers and I would run upstairs. I also knew very little
about running a home. In India, I didn't learn to cook or clean
the house, I simply passed exams. In the holidays at home my
mother and grandmother rather spoilt me. They didn't allow me
to do any household tasks. In those days when I prayed about
serving God I thought it meant just worshipping him all the
time.

When I came to this country my situation didn't change
much. If relatives came my mother-in-law or my mother looked
after them. I had to cook for Sewa and myself but I had no
experience of coping with larger groups. The first people who
came to us were the missionary friends from Pakistan and their
four children, whom we had met at Keswick. They had recently
arrived in Britain and had no friends or relatives here. They were
extremely lonely. I felt hesitant about inviting them, but did so,
remembering a friend explaining that inviting needy people
into your home in the name of the Lord Jesus is service. Alan
Thomas had also said to me once, 'Narindar, it's serving God
when you make a cup of tea for a stranger.'

I began to learn how to cook and clean and even found I
wanted to do so. To many Asians such menial tasks are only for
servants. Now the Lord had created in me a real desire to serve
him in this way. At first when visitors came to stay I prepared
meals beforehand because I was only just learning how to cope
with catering for a larger group of people than Sewa and me.

In this way I discovered that serving the Lord is not always
speaking from the front, giving Bible studies or being a leader
in the church. First of all we must learn to act in the capacity of
a servant. Not many Asians seem to like doing lowly tasks for
others. They like to be served but they haven't learned to serve.
We have to learn to be servants for the Lord before he can give

us any other task to do. And even if he does lead us into more upfront jobs, he still wants us to go on being servants.

So my first training point was in the kitchen. After we had entertained our missionary friends, I began welcoming other groups of Christians and non-Christians. We also started inviting home people who had been badly treated because they had become Christians. Their families would fight with them, sometimes physically. They tormented them in all sorts of other ways too. For instance, at a wedding or other celebration, a family may tell their Christian relative, 'You're not one of us any more,' or say to other guests, 'This is our sister. She has become a Christian. She is not like us.' A new believer who has not become strong in the Lord may answer back. Then sometimes a conflict starts which ends with the husband beating up his wife.

Two young women came to stay with us at first; one just for a few days, the other for several weeks. When they left us we lost touch with them. We had not yet learned the importance of following them up. From that beginning the ministry grew. There were only the two of us and we had three bedrooms so we had room for two or three needy people. Sometimes they came through friends, through them contacting me at school or through meetings we attended. If they had nowhere to go, Christian or non-Christian, our house was open to them. Those who came were battered, broken and abused. A number had endured incest. You name the sufferings women can undergo and we've cared for someone who has experienced them.

We also visited people in their own homes. Sometimes I went with Barbara Summers. When we were in Lozells, I went with Enid Dansey. I learned a lot from her. We entered quite poor homes. The poverty, the unhappiness was much the same as I had seen in India. The women were trodden upon, not able to do anything without asking their husbands. The children were unruly. The furniture was battered. Dirty plates littered the sitting room. An atmosphere of hopelessness pervaded the house. The women were often uneducated and their husbands unemployed and sometimes alcoholic. Many were ignorant about how to raise a family. As a consequence, the children were suffering too.

I didn't pray with them in the early days because I didn't know I should. However when I went out with Enid we never came back without having prayed. So I began to do so when visiting in Wolverhampton too. I began by visiting the homes of girls I taught in Sunday school and praying with them. Soon I began to do so in the company of non-believers too. I loved visiting Asian women, though I was inexperienced in how to minister to them. I soon learned to speak about Jesus. When they asked me who I was, what I did and so on I would say, 'I believe in the Lord Jesus Christ. He has given me peace.'

Soon some women put their trust in him themselves. I believe it happened because I was very loving to them. I'm not boasting about my own efforts. It was the Lord who gave me the love. They used to say, 'You love us so much.' Even this morning, Rani, who has been a Christian just one week said, 'I see something different in you. You're so Asian and yet so western as well. You love us in a way we don't often see these days.' God gave me this gift of love. Before coming to Christ I was an extremely reserved person. I hardly spoke to anyone. Now I am doing everything I didn't do when I was young. I asked God to make me bold like Paul and he has answered that prayer.

Everything was beginning to happen at once. There was so much to do and so much more we saw that needed doing. We longed to be of more help but there just wasn't time. All we could do was pray, 'Lord, show us the way.'

14

Needs in the Asian Community

It was becoming clear that there was a tremendous amount of work to do and that we needed more time. Life was so busy that sometimes I would go to bed at 2 or 3 a.m. and rise at 8 a.m. to reach school for nine o'clock. Desmond and Enid Dansey were encouraging us to evangelize. St Jude's leaders were asking us to bring more people like ourselves into the church.

One day Desmond, who was a Crosslinks missionary, said to us, 'Crosslinks are having a regional meeting in Wolverhampton at St Matthew's church. Would you come and give your testimonies?' We agreed, but on the day in question Sewa got cold feet. He said he had to go to Coventry on business. I'm not sure whether this was his own idea or whether his firm asked him to do so. Anyway he was not available to go to the meeting and Joan Salt took me instead.

Duncan McMann, the Crosslinks regional representative, the Thomases and some of our own church people were there. I alone had to give testimony for Sewa and myself. Sewa did eventually arrive but by that time the meeting was almost over. Before we had refreshments Duncan said, 'When Narindar was being prepared in India to come and work in this country, Sewa was being prepared here to come alongside her.' What I didn't know was that he had also said to Alan and Joan Thomas, 'If Sewa and Narindar ever feel called to serve the Lord full-time, Crosslinks would be interested.' At the same time, Sewa and I had been telling Desmond and Enid that wherever and whenever God gave us an opportunity to serve him, we wouldn't refuse it.

Life just took off after that. We were witnessing everywhere; with the Summers, with Enid and Desmond, at school, in Asian homes. Wherever there was an opportunity to speak for the Lord we took it. We would go and have prayer with Asian Christians and visit the families of the children I was teaching in Sunday school. We also called on Asians we had never met before but whom we heard were in need. We saw two or three people turning to Christ because we visited them and spoke about him. We continued to invite people to stay with us, especially young girls who had nowhere to go. As people heard that we were taking in such needy youngsters, they began to ask if we would have this or that one.

I was still living a western lifestyle in some ways till the Lord showed me I should identify more closely with those whom we were trying to help. I wore fashionable western clothes, trousers, blouses, and sweaters. And I particularly loved wearing the ankle-length dresses and skirts that were in fashion at the time. Sewa wore the same as western men. I hadn't worn saris or Punjabi suits for a long time. We had given up Asian dress even before we left the Asian community.

However, once, we went to London to give our testimonies at a Mission to London meeting. We stayed with Geoffrey and Barbara Rowland who had spent many years in Burma and were now working among Asians in Britain. Geoffrey is a godly and sensitive man. Before we left his house for the meeting, he said, 'Narindar, wouldn't it be nice if you wore an Asian outfit?' He didn't say openly, 'Identify with other Asians.' He was too tactful to do that. But I understood what he meant. I wore the only Punjabi suit I possessed for the meeting so as not to disobey a senior Christian. I didn't rebel as I had against the Asian community. I had learned to obey the teaching of my elders like the Thomases, and that blessed me.

When I returned home after the mission meeting I brought out all the material that I had not had made up. We had come to know a young woman about the same age as myself. Her husband was not a Christian and she needed friendship with someone like myself. So we started visiting her once a week. I soon discovered that she made and sold suits, so I asked her to make five or six for me.

Almost immediately after that I received a phone call from Marlin Summers asking me again to consider teaching Sunday school at his Asian fellowship. Now that I was willing to identify with Asians, God was opening the door. However when I went to the fellowship for the first time I didn't like it a bit. I sat in the meeting with my heart in my boots because the people were not my kind. Most of them were from poor backgrounds and their ways were different. Only one couple was from a Jat background, so I said to the Lord, 'Is this where you want me to serve you, Lord?' The reply in my mind was, 'Yes.' I struggled for a while to say, 'Right Lord, I will' but eventually I did. As a result I let go of all my Jat ways, all my expensive clothes. I stopped wearing saris because poorer people didn't do so. They wore Punjabi suits. Once when I went to visit a broken woman she looked at the rings on my fingers and said, 'Oh, sister, I don't have any jewellery.' So I stopped wearing jewellery. I obeyed what I saw as God's leading and the teaching of my seniors, though doing so broke me at times.

I also hid my academic qualifications. I realized that God had given me a higher degree of intelligence than most of these people but I made myself come down to their level so that they wouldn't be put off by me. I wanted them to learn to be God's servants. Foolish me, I didn't know that people do not become servants through human effort, but by God's grace.

I'd read the life story of the Apostle Paul in the New Testament and understood that he identified himself with the people to whom he was ministering and that inspired me. So from high caste I became low caste, from high intelligence I became the lowest of the low, so that no one would be jealous of me. I had been brought up to believe that as a Jat I was superior to other people but now, as I opened my heart to God, he gave me genuine love for low caste people. It was a miracle that only he could have performed. Now I saw them as my brothers and sisters who were in need of Christ. I also hid my education. If those I was trying to work with knew I had an MA they would cease to be open with me. Most of them had not gone beyond primary school. To most of my readers, qualifications don't matter as far as friendship is concerned. Everyone, prime ministers, doctors, or lorry drivers are qualified for the jobs God has given them to do. In some ways I made a mistake in hiding my education and abilities. I didn't heed Mrs Thomas when she said to me, 'Don't hide your qualifications. Most English people think Asians don't know anything. Make it clear that you are their equal in background, education and training. That way they will respect you.'

In our inexperience and zeal we made other mistakes too. Nobody explained to us that some people become Christians from ulterior motives. We were all for the Lord and thought all of them were genuine, spiritually seeking after God. Later we discovered that some people had identified with us for what they could get out of us; the love and attention they didn't receive from their families; and practical assistance too like baby-sitting, doing their shopping or helping in decorating the house. We never said, 'No,' to any request to help. Sometimes we endured abuse and insult so that people's souls might be saved. Even our closest friends didn't know the sacrifices we were making for the Lord's sake.

At the same time some of those people gave me tremendous love. I remember one woman saying to me, she's still a dear friend, 'When I saw you for the first time, I looked at you and thought, 'She's a lovely girl. I want to make friends with her.' She didn't know anything about me. I was thirty-two or thirty-three at the time but I looked younger. They used to say, 'You don't look very old. How old are you, twenty-five or twenty-six?' When we went to visit they would say, 'Welcome to our house.' They had no airs, they didn't show off. They lived often in old, rundown terraced houses in underprivileged parts of the city. Their homes were inadequately furnished. They were the simplest of simple people, yet they would offer me a melon or other food they could not really spare. I became very comfortable with them. Sometimes they commented that I was not very Asian in my ways. At other times they said, 'She's a very simple girl.' I had been simple in my ways from my teenage years. I loved simplicity from the moment I started spending time with God. I didn't need any pomp and show, unlike most of my community. Holiness was my aim. I found myself keeping simple in clothing and other habits so that I wouldn't in any way fall into temptation to spend time with worldly matters. I worked out these ideas for myself long before I became a Christian and, when I did, they were very useful.

15

All Nations

Every week that passed opened our eyes to more and more needs in the Asian community. I went to see a battered wife in one of the hostels run by the social services. It was so over-crowded that my heart broke. Four girls shared one room. One woman with two children was sharing with another family. The kitchen and bathroom were filthy. I could see that, although the hostels were refuges from physical harm and danger, there was no place for positive love. That's when I thought, 'Why couldn't we use our home as an open house? We could give them the love and care they don't receive at present.' I discussed it with Sewa and we realized we couldn't do so while we were both doing secular jobs. We needed to work full-time with these needy women.

One day when we were visiting Desmond and Enid we told them how we were feeling. 'To help meet the heart's cry of needy Asians, we long to work with them full-time. But how would we support ourselves and them if we did?' They listened carefully and then Desmond said, 'Why don't you go and talk to Crosslinks?'

Before doing so we felt we should speak to Alan and Joan Thomas. We were amazed to hear that Duncan McMann had already spoken to them about the possibility of our doing full-time Christian work. They would get in touch with him. Now we knew that we were in the line of God's will.

Although we were really doing missionary work already we had little understanding of the implications of full-time Chris-tian service. When we told Enid we were thinking of applying to Crosslinks she pointed out to them that it is hard enough for westerners to know the right way forward when they want to serve the Lord. How could Sewa and Narindar from another country, culture and religion be aware of what is required? She asked them to explain some of these requirements to us.

Duncan McMann, the Midlands Area Secretary for Crosslinks, came to see us. He seemed to have only one thing in mind, to listen to us. He had never been an overseas missionary. A problem with his health had prevented it. Yet he was a wonderful ambassador for the Lord right here in Britain. He was about fifty, a large man but gentle. Sewa used to call him 'the gentle giant.' At the same time Duncan was precise. When he chaired a meeting it ran to the exact minute advertised. He did everything in the correct order too. We felt he was like a sort of elder brother. He said to us, 'You can call me "Uncle-ji." ' He knew that that is the usual way young Asians address older men whom they respect. I didn't think of his visit as an interview, although that's what it was. When he was with you, you knew he was your friend. He stayed for a number of hours. I asked him lots of questions. Not about Crosslinks but about God. 'I want to know more about God,' I said, 'and Sewa does too.' I asked for Sewa because he was quiet in those days. Duncan didn't ask us many questions in return but we felt as if he knew all about us. Gordon Fyldes, the Other Faiths Secretary, in London, also interviewed us. Both men were skilful and tactful, humble and loving. They were extremely competent but what impressed me most was the love and care we received from them both. It was far beyond what duty required. Even after Crosslinks had accepted us, during our training and later on when we were back in the work in Wolverhampton, they would phone us to ask how we were. Duncan would also make special trips to see how we were progressing.

Duncan told us, 'You are sufficiently qualified through your education and work experience to go to Bible college. I suggest you apply to All Nations Christian College in Hertfordshire for two years' missionary training. Meanwhile Crosslinks will consider an application from you to be one of their missionaries. If you return to Wolverhampton afterwards, you'll be doing all that you are doing now, and more. But you'll have much greater knowledge and understanding of how to work for God.'

We were eager to go ahead and completed the application forms for Crosslinks. Shortly after that we heard that they had accepted us as missionaries. Now to apply to All Nations. We found the forms we had to fill in quite complicated. We didn't understand some of the questions about basic doctrinal beliefs, such as 'How do you understand God as father.' No one had ever yet discussed them with us. Thankfully Duncan came over and helped us to answer them. The college offered us places from September 1982, but because Sewa needed some surgery, we didn't start our course until a year later.

Towards the end of 1982, an Asian Christian family with two children whom we had known for many months had to leave their joint family home because of conflicts with the husband's father. We had two empty bedrooms. We had committed ourselves, our home and all our possessions to the Lord so we opened our home to them. When we welcomed them, we believed we were welcoming Christ. We became a joint family in him. They stayed with us for two years. In the second year they were alone because we had gone to All Nations.

St Jude's paid our tuition fees for All Nations and we paid for the rest. Many of the church members were fully behind us. They wrote to us, phoned to see how we were getting on and prayed for us regularly. They encouraged us greatly. I went to Bible college with the same flame still burning. How could I learn more about God? The practical training was rather irrelevant. We were already working as evangelists in Wolverhampton and the college didn't have experience of the sort of work we were doing. We learned a great deal academically though, especially about the Bible. I learned how to prepare a sermon too. However I longed for deeper teaching on holiness. I used to say to my personal tutors, John Martin and Vera Sinton, 'I want to know more about God.' I felt frustrated about that. Nobody seemed able to teach me what I wanted. It spoilt my joy at Bible college. I thought that, just as I had first learned about Jesus through the Thomases and then Colin Urquhart, others must be able to teach me more. Only after many years did I come to realize that nobody can teach you about going deeper into the Lord. It comes through perseverance in prayer and personal searching. However, nobody ever told me that. I wonder if they were afraid I would take offence? Sometimes I felt like giving up on Christianity as I had on Sikhism. Thank God I didn't. I'm still searching though for more of God through praying and reading. Each morning Sewa and I spend time reading the Bible and trying to come to grips with its teaching in a deep way.

I learned a good deal through my relationships with the other students. I became great friends with a student from Japan. She had nowhere to go one Christmas, so I asked her to spend it with us at home. She just thanked me gently. Weeks went by and she didn't say anything definite about coming. So one day I said to her, 'You haven't said yet whether you will definitely come to us for Christmas. We would like you to. Tell us how you feel about it.' She said to me, 'Narindar, you asked me in a casual manner. You must know how we Asians respond to that sort of invitation. I would only come if you really pressed me, saying, "Come on, you've got to come." ' Her response shocked me into realizing how western I had become in my thinking since I came to live in Britain. It challenged me to immerse myself again in Asian ways of thinking. Without doing so, I wouldn't be able to identify with the people to whom I wanted to witness. In particular, needy Asian people only respond to your attempts at friendship if you make it obvious in a forceful yet gentle, loving way that you do really care.

In 1982, we had felt we should buy a bigger house so that we could take in more needy women and girls. Already Sewa had sometimes to go and sleep in the garage. As it happened Richard Cottrell, a member of St Jude's, was an estate agent. He took responsibility for the sale of our house. However it hung fire for nearly two years. Finally someone made an offer far below our asking price. We had still another year to complete at Bible college. Nevertheless we agreed to sell them the house. Then I panicked. Where would we live now? But Sewa said, 'We put our house up for sale in the name of the Lord Jesus Christ. Let it be sold. The Lord will provide. Stop worrying.' And he did provide. A friend arranged for us to rent a house belonging to a housing association. The family who had been with us in the Sedgley house moved with us. We were now living in an extremely needy area of Wolverhampton. A prostitute used the house next door to ours. Prostitutes also occupied a block of flats opposite. We had known of Asian girls turning to prostitution before but now seeing one living next door we understood more of the life they led. One night a horrendous fight happened in front of our house. People shouted, screamed and swore. The baby next door began to cry. When I came out of our house the following morning I had to step across a big pool of dried blood. I had been so sheltered all my life that it was a shock to be exposed to such activities. Nevertheless I knew these were the sort of women God was calling me to serve.

We now began searching for a large house where we could carry on the work to which we believed God was calling us. Richard was most helpful, warning us against one or two houses that we had thought might be suitable. He told us they were in poor condition. Before long, Catherine Field told us of a house that just seemed to meet our needs It was large, divided into two flats. The downstairs flat had a sitting room, bedroom, dining room, kitchen and bathroom. The upper flat had similar facilities including three bedrooms and a two-bedroomed attic on a separate floor above. We knew that we could easily convert the building back to one house with living quarters downstairs and several bedrooms above. The one problem was that the asking price was more than we could afford. We didn't know what to do. Some people said, 'Perhaps, Sewa and Narindar, you haven't understood the Lord's calling.' But we were sure God had called us to have a larger house. Otherwise why would he have led us the way he had? We told Richard about the house and he said, 'How about if the price comes down a bit?' It turned out that Pentecostal Christians owned the house. They already knew of our plans, as did many Christians in Wolverhampton. When Richard spoke to them they said, 'We will let them have the house for their work for whatever price they can afford.' To our amazement, when we named a figure £5000 below what they were originally asking, they accepted it. They also said they would leave behind all the carpets, curtains and other fittings. When the estate agents agreed to forgo a deposit, we could scarcely believe it.

Now we needed a mortgage. One evening when I went to Douglas and Catherine's prayer meeting, I told those present about our need. After the prayer time a Christian brother spoke to me, saying, 'I work for a building society. Maybe I can help you. I explained our dilemma and he said, 'Send Sewa to the building society tomorrow.' Sewa didn't usually take the initia-

tive in those days. However when I went home and told him
about the conversation he said, 'I don't mind going for God's
sake.'

The next morning Sewa did so and explained our situation.
We were at college and though we had some money it wasn't
enough for the mortgage. We planned to use the house as an
open house for needy Asian women. After discovering that we
were reliable and trustworthy they arranged a mortgage on
terms that we could afford to pay.

Two weeks later we went back to college with the business
in the hands of the solicitors. We were full of thanksgiving. By
November 1984, the house was ours. The family who stayed
with us saw to the removal of all our possessions and moved in.
We instructed them right from the start not to refuse anyone
needing shelter. So even before Sewa and I returned in July 1985
the work had started.

I had seen God take the initiative in my life once again. He
had been with me in my childhood and teenage years. He
planned my marriage. He led me to teach in a school with a
Christian headmistress. He drew me to himself. Now in the
provision of this house I was continuing to see his hand at work.
We didn't know how to conduct all the business arrangements
required. We came from another background, culture and faith.
We had been rejected by our families and former Sikh friends.
We alone could not have done all that was required. But God
had done it through our Christian brothers and sisters.

16

Discernment and Church Politics

A year or two before we went to Bible college, some Asian
Christians from an Asian fellowship in Wolverhampton that
worshipped on Sunday evenings, had started attending St
Jude's morning service. Their young people in particular pre-
ferred it to the traditional Asian style service. By 1984 these
people had become dissatisfied with their leader altogether and
left the group. Others left too and didn't go to any other place
of worship instead.

When we came home from college for our second Christmas,
the breakaway group had nowhere to go for their Christmas
celebrations. We felt sorry for them and said to each other, 'Why
couldn't they meet in our house? It's big enough.' So we issued
an invitation that they accepted. Forty or fifty people squeezed
into our middle room downstairs on Christmas Eve. They held
a service of worship with Punjabi hymns and readings from the
Christmas story. Following this, we served refreshments.

We had no idea of doing anything further. However, before
we returned to college some of the Asian Christians came to ask
us if they could have regular Punjabi services in our house on
Sunday afternoons. We said to the couple who were living there,
'It's up to you.' They agreed and the new meeting started. We
were trying to walk as the Lord led and we thought that this
would be a means of showing our love. Later we realized that
we would have been wiser to have given it more thought before
agreeing. We paid a costly price for our decision. Had we known
the Bible as we do now, I don't think we would have become
involved. We would have heeded Paul's teaching in Hebrews
13:17 about obeying one's leader even if he makes mistakes. At
the same time we realize that occasionally a leader falls into real
error, disobeying God or behaving in an immoral way. Then we
may have to leave a church rather than submit to the vicar or
pastor. But we should only do so after seeking God earnestly in

prayer so that we make a decision in line with his will.

The result was a lot of trouble in Wolverhampton, though by the time it erupted we had returned to college. Some people were angry with us for what we had done, though Mr and Mrs Thomas were still loving and supportive. Yet they must have thought, 'Oh, what are these people up to?' We didn't see that we were doing anything wrong. We tried to bring reconciliation between the breakaway group and their former leader, but failed. Then we began to feel, 'If the group won't go back, someone must pastor them. What about us doing so?' We loved them and wanted to see them grow as Christians. Eventually the college let us drive home from Ware to Wolverhampton for several weekends to lead a service for the Asian group, though it was against the college rules. I'm truly grateful because if they hadn't allowed us to do so, I think I might have left college. After a while we talked to Desmond Dansey and he agreed to come and preach to the Asian group on Sundays.

However, because the group had no stable leadership they soon fell out amongst themselves. They knew that we had held prayer meetings asking the Lord to bring men and women to himself and to show us how to disciple them so they decided to do the same. With little experience, they began experimenting with prophecy. One woman gave a disturbing prophecy that was very much against Asian custom. She said that her husband and the wife of another member of the group would die and the surviving partners marry each other. This upset a number of the members who felt that an injustice had been done. They wanted us to ask the two to repent. Sewa tackled the man concerned saying, 'Look brother, what you did wasn't right.' Sewa loved him and his family and so talked gently, but the man simply said, 'The prophecy was given. What are you going to do about it?' No one was willing for reconciliation and so the Fellowship split. One of the two groups began asking God to let them take over the house and prevent our coming back to it. They planned to make a Pentecostal church their base. Incidentally the prophecy never came true.

Meanwhile we had begun our last term at All Nations, fully expecting to return to work in Wolverhampton afterwards. But problems arose because of what we had done to help the breakaway Asian group. Various people began writing to the college and to Crosslinks saying we ought not to come back. Even members of St Jude's began to feel we shouldn't return until the difficulties had blown over. Crosslinks wondered if they should send us to Manchester. At the same time the group that had not left our Fellowship began saying, 'We will not go to any church unless you come back to St Jude's.' Our sympathies were with them because at the time we felt they were right. Looking back however, we sometimes wonder if they blackmailed us into returning to them. Nevertheless, there were three families from a non-Christian background who had come to know the Lord, and five nominal Christian families who needed pastoring. Of course, the house was already operational.

In the midst of the confusion we did receive one letter that warmed our hearts. Geoffrey, the missionary who had suggested I wear Indian dress for the Mission to London meeting, wrote, 'Many churches in many places want you to work with them. There are few missionaries of your background. Remember your original calling is to Wolverhampton. So you honour your calling and the Lord will bless you.' Finally through the intervention of the vicar with whom Geoffrey worked, who spoke with both Mr Thomas and Crosslinks, we did go back. Even then on the day we were leaving college we received a letter from one person telling us not to return.

As soon as we returned we assumed permanent leadership of the Punjabi/English Fellowship. Not only did we use our middle room for the worship meeting, we also had Sunday school for the children in other rooms. Sometimes Mr Thomas came to preach to us. The number attending the Fellowship grew. By October 1985 our room was no longer large enough, so St Jude's allowed us to meet in their hall instead. Some of our newcomers were ready for baptism. We felt the symbolism of total immersion was important for them, so Mr Thomas approached the local Brethren Assembly. They were glad to welcome us. One Sunday afternoon Mr Thomas baptized ten adults. The church was packed. Afterwards our Brethren friends provided refreshments.

The group continued to grow but early in 1986 one or two members began to ask us to do things differently. Our aim has always been to integrate with the main church body as far as we can. But the dissatisfied members of the Punjabi/English Fellowship were accusing the English members of St Jude's of being racist. At the same time these very people made a variety of excuses for not getting to know anyone in the main church. However, what they suggested was not acceptable either to us or to St Jude's. Nor was it appropriate for the new Christians in the group. When we said so, those making the difficulties shouted at us and refused to listen. They felt that they knew best and demanded that we obey them. But we had been appointed leaders of the Fellowship and couldn't with a good conscience do what they were asking. We continued to love them and try to reach some kind of reconciliation. However they demanded that either we did what they asked or they would leave. They were not willing to sit down and talk matters out with us. They simply threw accusations at us, saying that we didn't love them and the church didn't either.

One other difficulty we faced was that of jealousy. Our work was going ahead and we were seeing people come to the Lord. Some church members, both English and Asian, who hadn't had such a ministry didn't support what we were doing. Instead they actively worked against us: talking about us behind our backs and seeking to destroy the work we were trying to build up. I have discovered that this is not unusual when some church members meet success in their ministry and others don't. We need to pray for Christians to be willing to accept whatever position God puts them in rather than always seeking the limelight.

Sadly, we had to let the dissatisfied people go, and they took three or four families with them to start a group in another church. This was the first time we found ourselves at loggerheads with other Asian Christians. We found it difficult to understand why we were going through such a struggle, but we determined not to waver from the guidance we believed the Lord had given us. Later, we understood that such a situation is not uncommon in the Asian community. Certain members become increasingly demanding and want their needs met at the expense of others. Sometimes I think one needs to be the archangel Michael to have the strength and energy to work with them.

Some of those left behind gave us difficulties too. Those from Hindu, Sikh and Muslim backgrounds often wanted all our attention. We were expecting them to welcome new members. However, now I look back, I can see they just wanted us in their pockets. If we gave new people attention, they were jealous. One woman even asked me accusingly, 'Do you love Kamla more than you love me?' Then the new ones would say, 'We're not coming to this church because all of you have been together right from the start and we're not welcome.' Sewa and I found it all very difficult. Everybody wanted our personal attention but we couldn't be everywhere. It was the duty of the more established families to welcome the new ones but instead they were antagonistic. They felt the fewer their numbers, the more attention they would receive from us.

We hadn't withdrawn from our goal of reaching new families, though this first upset within the Fellowship unsettled me a lot. But with God's strength Sewa and I determined to walk on the path on which we believed the Lord had set us. We visited families I had had contact with in my teaching days, and others whom we heard were in need. Sometimes we spent four or five hours with one family. We often left the house at eight o'clock in the morning and didn't return until midnight. Some of these families committed their lives to the Lord Jesus and joined the Fellowship.

Meanwhile members of St Jude's, though supportive, didn't know what they could do to help us. It's pioneering work and it's tough. But they loved us and prayed for us and some said, 'Tell us what we can do and we'll do it.' As a result, a group of English young people from the main congregation began to come regularly to the Punjabi/English Fellowship on Sunday afternoons and lead us in English singing. Paul, the Thomases eldest son, played the guitar. Mr and Mrs Thomas also joined us regularly. Then on Mondays they would phone asking for prayer topics for the Tuesday afternoon ladies' group. Later, Mr Thomas began to give communion at the Punjabi/English fellowship once a month. If we had to go away to speak or for any other reason he also preached through interpretation. The Punjabi congregation did not yet know enough about the Christian faith to teach Sunday school effectively. So five or six English ladies came and took the children out for teaching or looked after the babies. There was no language barrier there, as, once children go to school, they soon become fluent in English.

After the service we would invite people home for a cup of tea. These visitors included Asians and English people and particularly any new enquirers who had come to the service. It was exciting to see people of different cultures mingling in this way.

Some people may ask why we needed a separate Asian service when there were plenty of opportunities for worship in the main church. Many of the Asian Christians are uneducated and do not understand English. Some women, who came from India and Pakistan as adults, have never been to school so they don't read even Punjabi and don't know any English. Older men can't read and write English, even if they speak a little. These people would be totally at sea in an English service. We do encourage Asians with good English to join the services in English, though even then, a sermon in one's first language goes deeper than in any other.

Soon we found we needed a minibus, as people were coming to the Fellowship from all over Wolverhampton. Some of the women who came with little children and without their husbands had special difficulties. Because of the cultural restrictions on women in Asian society, these husbands objected to their wives travelling on public transport. They also made a fuss because their wives were not at home to provide meals when they wanted them. One man even beat his wife up because the buses were delayed and she arrived home later than he expected. People coming by bus from the other side of town had to catch two different ones and, as they are infrequent on Sundays, they sometimes waited two or three hours at the bus stops. Children became fretful, especially when it was raining. All these hindrances can spoil someone's joy. We managed to acquire a very, very old minibus. Brothers in the Punjabi/English Fellowship who were skilled in mechanics renovated it. However, it was never reliable. Through Crosslinks, seven partnership churches supported us. When they heard through our prayer letter about our need, many of them sent donations for a better bus. Within a few months we were able to buy a brand new one. Everyone in the Fellowship was overjoyed at their generosity.

In 1987 Mr and Mrs Thomas retired. Howell and Jean Davies, who had been missionaries in Uganda succeeded them. Because of their experience, they understood about relating to people of a different culture. Even so, the first time we met Howell he wanted to know more about Asians. He had a white beard that he used to stroke when he was thinking about something. He had a good sense of humour, but when anyone talked seriously, he would quietly give them his full attention. Howell used to say, 'I want to learn from you,' and I would say, 'But I want to learn from you.' He was such a good teacher. When he was preaching, you knew you would learn something about how to live a Christian life. Jean had been born in India, of missionary parents, so to some extent she understood Indian ways. She was a plump person, and motherly just as Joan Thomas was. They would both put their arms round you and hug you when you needed a little encouragement. Jean Davies was very warm and always ready to give me advice if I needed it, though she never gave it in a way that made you feel she was talking down to you. From both the Thomases and the Davieses I learned humility. They had gone through trials and temptations during their lives and over many years they had learned to walk closely with the Lord. I learned much from them about how to live my own Christian life. I missed the Davieses very much when they retired in 1993.

Even though Mr and Mrs Thomas were so loving we still felt like second-class citizens as far as most of the rest of the church was concerned. Howell had our position affirmed in writing by the Parochial Church Council. He also made sure the treasurer of the main church organized the finances of the Punjabi/English Fellowship properly. He took a most important step when he set up an Action Group to oversee our work, give us adequate support, and liaise with the main body of the church. We were so busy visiting from door to door that we had never given much thought to the way the main church supported us. The Action Group consists of ten or twelve people and meets three times a year. It guides us, advises us, prays for us and sees to any work that needs doing for the Punjabi/English Fellowship. Of course, we keep them closely in touch with what we are doing. I feel every church with workers involved in Asian outreach should have an Action group. It's impossible for the PCC or board of elders to have the time or opportunity to deal fully with what affects such workers. They have too much else to do in the general administration of the church. We wish we had had an Action group in the church when we first started to work with it. It might have avoided some of the misunderstandings and hurts that arose.

Howell also suggested that we become lay readers and we were licensed in 1988. Since then Sewa has taken part in the English language services on a regular basis. He both leads services and preaches sometimes. This is remarkable because he was a Jat Sikh. Jats are the highest caste in Sikhism. They are proud, often stubborn and usually fanatically devoted to the Sikh faith. They are almost impossible to reach with the gospel. Sewa's conversion and leadership in the Christian church are miracles of God's grace.

One very important factor in our work has been the stable situation in the church. The Thomases and the Davieses both stayed for several years. When a new minister comes to a church in an Asian area, it takes him some time to come to grips with the situation. I feel a frequent change of leader is a disadvantage to a church wanting to reach out to people who come from cultures other than his own. I think a leader should stay at least ten years if he wishes to create a truly multi-racial church, which is stable and able to reach out into the community.

This point needs understanding by missionary societies too. A number of workers, like ourselves, are sponsored by them. They have policies that are practical overseas, but not necessarily valid in this country. Over the years, shorter contracts for missionaries have become common. These people go overseas, fulfil a three-year contract and then come home. Some societies try to introduce the same rules in Britain. Sewa and I feel this is not adequate. Asian work is ongoing and extremely tough. You must work twenty-four hours a day if you want to see results. Even five years is not enough to establish the work and give the new Christians security. Building up trust and confidence takes years, sometimes as many as fifteen, for both the host church and the emerging Asian Christian group.

Churches and missionary agencies often seem to put the main emphasis on winning converts and starting Asian fellow-ships. They need to realize that the work is not complete when this happens. Discipling converts is so important and takes years. The new believers have burnt their boats as far as their old extended family system is concerned. They very much need to find a new stability in the Lord. Nor are all their other problems solved when they become Christians. In fact, some, like how to arrange marriages for their children and look after elderly parents, are just beginning. Converts have to be taught to depend on the Lord to meet every need. If they are not, they may easily fall by the wayside and go back to their old faith or be drawn away by false teaching. They have to be loved and nurtured carefully by their leaders. Some onlookers have felt that the leaders were exercising too much 'control'. But the truth is that, without careful teaching and supervision in their early years as Christians, they fall away. It takes years before they learn to depend on the Lord for all their needs.

Sewa and I have found it important to have a plan for discipling Asian converts. It is also important that workers among Asians are supported by wise, caring church leaders with an effective teaching ministry, who stay in the church for a good number of years. Much damage can be done by inexperienced, insensitive or indifferent leaders. Sewa and I have been grateful for the caring and capable vicars we have had in both the Thomases and the Davieses.

17

The Open House

The open house work continued. Before we went to Bible college, girls came and stayed with us for six or seven months. They received an allowance from the social services but we charged them nothing. There was no one to guide either them or us. They just spent the money, often on clothes they didn't really need. When we returned from All Nations and started the work full time, we were advised to ask the girls to pay for their food and room. Otherwise all the expenses come out of our own pocket. We are not a registered charity. If we were, we would receive more funding but we would rather forego this than put the girls in danger. Sometimes it is essential that others do not know where they are. Because we are a family, we provide them with everything they need. We don't receive from them the amount we spend out, but we don't tell anyone. And God does always provide.

We had only been back from college for a week when a social worker brought a depressed and badly bruised woman to us. Her mother-in-law and two children came too. Her husband had beaten her so badly that the blue marks on her body brought tears to my eyes. As a result she was terrified of men. Sewa and I comforted her and after the mother-in-law had assured herself that her daughter-in-law was in good hands, she returned home. The children were afraid too. They would never go to the door in case their father had arrived. Though no one except social workers knew what we were doing, somehow he came to hear where his wife was. He sent several threatening messages including some saying he intended to come with a knife and kill Sewa. After a few weeks the council gave the woman a house. She was a dedicated Sikh and though we talked to her about Jesus, she left without inviting him into her life. After a while we heard that her husband had come to live with her. But once again he treated her badly. One day he burnt down the house in anger, and again the social services looked after her. They moved her to another council house. She seemed happy then with her children and gradually we lost touch with her.

Ever since then, women and girls have been coming and going. We called our home an open house rather than a hostel. We didn't want to be identified with the hostels run by the social services that we felt were such inadequate substitutes for homes for desperate and lonely women. However, for the sake of meeting our costs we had to register as such. For all other purposes we talk about an open house.

The first battered wife had scarcely left when someone from Birmingham brought us Kamla, a girl of seventeen. Her mother had died when she was nine years old. When she was fifteen, her father went to India with her younger sister. At home, certain men, her sister's husband in particular, made sexual advances to her. In fear of him, she left home and went to a hostel in Birmingham. There a gang of boys got to know about her and manipulated her into prostitution. Eventually she met Ken, a Christian man, and told him, 'I want to get out of this life but I don't know how.' He tried to find a Christian family to take her in, but nobody wanted her. In desperation he took her to the Lozells bookshop. Desmond and Enid contacted us. Her story was so sad that I fell in love with her as soon as she came. We sat and talked as if we had known each other for years. Her experiences had been so painful that she needed continual comfort. I loved her because she was the victim of circumstances. Sometimes we would sit talking all night long about the suffering she had endured. One night she said to me, 'Look Narindar, it's getting light.' We went to bed and I left a note for Sewa saying, 'Don't wake me early in the morning. I went to bed at 3 a.m.' That happened night after night. She had become used to night life and couldn't go to sleep early. I had to spend the time with her to convince her that we did care and that she was not on her own. It was tough for me. Sewa would say, 'You must look after yourself otherwise you will be ill.' After she had been with us for a few months we talked to her about the Lord Jesus Christ and prayed for her to have peace about the past. She came to the point where she wanted to give her life to him. It wasn't just through our efforts.

Mrs Thomas loved her too. She was the only one in the church who knew her story. After what she had been through, the young woman wondered if she could ever be of any use to anyone. Mrs Thomas invited her to help her in the toddlers' Sunday school and so gave her some self respect. Sewa looked after her social needs outside the home. Only I could spend time with her at home. Sewa couldn't do so because of the cultural taboos in Asian society about relationships between men and women. She didn't leave us till she was nearly twenty-one.

After Kamla's conversion, another girl came to stay. Farah was from a Muslim background and again she had a sad story. She lived with us for three years. While these two girls were with us, battered wives and others who had been ill-treated also came and went. After they had been with us for a while most of them gave their lives to Jesus, though they didn't come to St Jude's church. I'm still in touch with one of them. She lives in a council flat and says, 'I still believe in Jesus Christ.'

Other needy young women came to stay after the first two girls moved on. I determined that everyone who came should turn to the Lord. Of course, in the end that is the Holy Spirit's work, but I left undone nothing that I could do. I used every gift God had given me for those who came. Sacrificial giving in the power of the Holy Spirit is what brought them to Christ.

However, some people didn't want to come and stay with us. After all these years I'm just discovering why. It's the nature of most human beings to resent new people joining a close, knit group. I found out that those who had lived with us for some time would ask the new people questions they didn't want to answer. They would also comment on their appearance and actions and laugh at them in an offensive way. This upset the prospective newcomers.

In ten years, one hundred and seventy women and girls have been through our house. Some stayed only for hours, others for weeks and some for three or four years. The women come with physical, emotional and spiritual problems, but the Lord Jesus brings them into wholeness, though the process is normally very painful. We have spoken to most of them about how he can be their Saviour. Some have accepted him and been truly liberated from their past hurts, although the process of discipling and teaching has to go on for many, many years.

Some of the women and girls we took in had been involved in prostitution. In the late 1950s and early 1960s many Asians came to the area from India. Most were from rural backgrounds with little education and no skills. Since this is an industrial area, most of them found it difficult to adjust to their new environment and the values of the West. Afraid of change, they held on to their own traditions and culture. At the same time they were not readily accepted by the host community because of their different language, culture and colour. So they congregated together to preserve their identity.

Today Wolverhampton has about 30,000 Asians. The unemployment in this area is high. In 1993 it was about 30 per cent. With such problems there has been a steady rise in alcohol abuse and wife battering that has led to a breakdown in family life.

The next generation is born into this climate. Growing up in a western world with British schooling, they are torn between their parents' traditional values and British culture which they see as 'free'. They see their British counterparts doing things their parents forbid them to and are envious. However, if they rebel and leave home, they do not know how to handle the sudden freedom without the support of an extended family.

Most Indian parents still want to arrange their daughters' marriages, according to tradition. In the early years of Asian immigration most girls accepted this as there was no alternative. The woman has a distinct role in Asian society as a housewife and mother. Parents train girls for this role from childhood. When they marry, they leave for their husband's home. However, as time has gone by, attitudes in the host community have changed. It is now easier for girls in Britain to refuse arranged marriages. In addition, many Asian families consider daughters a burden. Mothers and older sisters-in-law may go out to work full-time. Girls may then have to sweep the house, do the washing, cook the meals, and attend to all the household chores from the time they are about nine years old. Often parents swear at them for the slightest hint of misbehaviour. Parents feel aggrieved that they have to pay a dowry, sometimes of thousands of pounds, when the daughters marry. Often a family makes a girl feel guilty about this and starves her of affection. Consequently they end up with low self-esteem. They desperately want acceptance, often rebelling against their own culture. In their vulnerability, they fall prey to Asian men who take advantage of them. After a while many end up in prostitution or drug carrying. Once in the grip of their pimps, they become increasingly frightened. With no one to turn to, they are unable to escape. It takes great courage and a lot of help for such girls to break free. When they came to us, it took months of struggle to help them.

Some girls didn't come to us from prostitution. They just rebelled against their families' harsh treatment and ran away. They were then likely to end up on the street. In order to prevent this we took them in. Girls came to us from a variety of backgrounds but all of them were broken and rejected, depressed, angry and frustrated. Between them they had all sorts of problems: prostitution, drugs, depression, desertion by boyfriends. One girl even tried to commit suicide. Many Asian and English onlookers thought we were enjoying the work. In reality we suffered a great deal, without anyone alongside to support us. At the same time we were aware that our help and protection was insufficient. Women needed the Lord Jesus Christ: his help, his security and his grace to calm their troubled hearts.

In the early days of the work some girls came to the Lord but others only wanted the material benefits they could receive from us. They arrived insecure, unhappy, emotionally unstable and often physically unwell. They also had deep spiritual needs. I spent most of my nights talking, listening and then bringing Jesus into the situation wherever I could. It is not uncommon for some girls to take the time and attention of three workers because their needs are so great. They responded warmly to the love and affection they received, probably for the first time in their lives. However, when their need had been met, they began to view us as they had their parents. They still remembered their harshness vividly and rebelled against it. At first they were happy to obey the rules of the house. We had to have these to live together and to create a family atmosphere for them. For instance we expected them to help with household duties such as cooking, washing up and keeping the house tidy. However as they recovered and began to feel secure they rebelled against doing these jobs. Some of them had been so verbally abused as children that they resented the slightest hint of correction from us too. They would begin to compare our home and lifestyle with that of their parents, usually to the latter's disadvantage. We always tried to bring reconciliation between rebellious girls and their parents, but often had to leave time to sort things out.

At first we only took in two girls and they would readily accept Christ as their Saviour. Later we began to have four or five at a time but this gave us headaches. They wanted to break every rule in the house, and us to capitulate to their every demand. They would also fight among themselves. In 1991 I became seriously ill and since then we have taken only one or two girls at the most. We don't just provide a roof over their heads like many hostels. We want the girls' needs met in every way. Sometimes we arrange for them to go to college so that they learn a skill with which they can support themselves. We found one girl was musical, so we arranged for her to have piano lessons.

Not only did we have girls and women in our home, we also went out to the homes of those who had returned to live in the community. And to other needy families also. We didn't just preach the gospel, we served them in any way they needed in order to share the love of Jesus. I went into the homes of semi-prostitutes, swept their floors, did their cooking, washed their dishes, took their dirty clothes to the laundry. Sometimes I even brought their clothes home to iron. I never let them know I had been a Jat Sikh. If they knew, they would never have allowed me to do those jobs. I didn't divulge my background ever. I went to every length possible to show the love of Christ and to help them come to the point of receiving him as their Saviour. It paid off.

Sewa and I often had a laugh about all the things they expected us to do: baby-sit for their children or take them to school, teach them, remove their furniture when their own family wouldn't help them, go with them to social services. To some extent those who had lived with us had conformed again to the community's way of living. Rather than coming to us to see if they could help with new people, they were expecting Sewa and me to go on doing the same jobs for them. One woman even went so far as to say, 'Sewa and Narindar, you must spend a day with our children once a week, and a day with the family.' That's how it was with every family. They all wanted Sewa and me for two days. Yet they came reluctantly to Bible study. I see now that their hearts were not truly for God but only for what they could get from him; and from Sewa and me. Meanwhile they expected us to live off air. They didn't expect us two to have any needs. In India, godly people live in the jungle, don't have houses and are extremely poor. They thought we should be the same. When they saw Sewa and me inviting others into our home they became jealous. Although some of them had become Christians through us and the work of the Punjabi/English service, they slowly started turning against us because we were going to new people. They wanted us all to themselves and were not willing to share us with others.

At the same time we had more difficulties with members of the Punjabi/English fellowship. They all wanted to be leaders though they were unqualified and without experience. We had thought they were genuinely seeking to serve the Lord, but later we discovered that most of them were there for their own ends. We were very innocent, never doubting that people wanted to give God everything. But they took advantage of us because we were not cunning or clever. We didn't hide anything from them about our personal circumstances, not even how much money we received. We thought if we were open about everything, it would enable us to work more closely with them. However, because we had imbibed western attitudes, we failed to remember that in Asian culture positions are given not on grounds of ability but for reasons of prestige. Gaining prestige was the aim of many of the members of the Fellowship. One man in particular wanted to preach, though he could only speak a few words of English and was not really literate in Punjabi either. He wanted to be upfront receiving all the credit, being applauded and glorified, while Sewa did all the propping up from behind.

In 1987 Susan came to help us for six months. We had studied together at Bible college. She had applied to a missionary society for overseas service but was not accepted. When she visited us after this disappointment, I said to her, 'Come on, let's work together.' And we did. She visited with me, helped to drive and was a good all-round assistant. She had an excellent sense of humour but was also serious about her commitment to Christ and her service for him. She had a real heart for Asian women and after her experience with us went on to work in an Asian area of Bradford. She has continued to serve the Lord faithfully amongst Asian women and is now in Derby.

As time went on we found the needs of the girls in the hostel, the visiting in Asian homes and the pastoring of the Punjabi/English Fellowship taking up more and more time. And there was so much more we could have done. I said to Howell and Jean that we needed a younger person to come alongside us as Susan had, someone who would be one with us in aim and purpose. Jean understood that I wanted someone really dedicated and she said, 'You want another Narindar with you. But there aren't many who will give themselves totally as you do.' 'I know' I said, 'but I'm praying about it and I believe the Lord will give me one.' And would you believe it, one day, at a Crosslinks conference, we met the leader of the Finnish Lutheran team that was working in Britain. We told him how overwhelmed with work we were. He said in return, 'I think perhaps I could find a volunteer from Finland to help you.' That was how Katri came to us in 1989. She was not yet twenty-one and took a year out of her university course to work with us. Amazingly, away there in Finland, God spoke to her about the need of Asian people who had emigrated to Europe. She asked him to send her to an Asian couple involved in missionary work alongside whom she could work. When the opening came she knew it was God's call to her. Katri was blond, slim, gently spoken and gifted in music. The young people in the Punjabi/English fellowship warmed to her immediately. She had such ability to come alongside them and listen to them. She led Bible studies with them, taught them new Christian songs as well as taking them to suitable secular activities such as the cinema or a shopping trip. At Christmas she took them to a pantomime. But she was also ready to sit and listen to adult workers who had more experience of serving the Lord than she did.

Katri and I took to each other immediately. We were both work-orientated and spent long hours visiting or listening to women in our home. As we came to know each other we grew to love one another deeply. We would pray together, fast together and laugh together. Sewa and I had fun helping her with her English and teaching her to drive on the left hand side of the road. Sewa said she and I were always giggling together; and we were. Singing and laughter were Katri's trade marks. We had a joyful house when she was around.

I missed Katri a great deal when she returned to Finland in 1990. However, while she was with us, we talked about the possibility of having an evangelistic team during the summer. In August 1990, through Katri, a team of six young people came from Finland for four weeks. A team of five, from Britain, followed in September. Then in 1991 another team of six came from Finland. Three of the girls remained for three months as part of their Bible college training. In succeeding years we had other teams and found them a helpful addition to our normal outreach programme. Each morning we taught them about the different Asian religions they would encounter. We also showed them films of Indian festivals and explained how Asian culture differed from western. In the afternoons and evenings they went visiting, sometimes door-to-door, sometimes in Asian homes, drinking tea with the family and talking with them. One or two of us always stayed behind to pray for the visiting team and make a meal for their return. We never sent them out unless a team at home supported them in prayer.

We were encouraged by the many contacts that the teams made. But apart from Sewa and myself, no one in the church offered to help with follow-up so we lost many of them. Following people up is hard work and no individual can do so with more than a few families. If any church is going to have a visiting campaign its members must commit themselves beforehand to follow-up work. When we saw the reluctance of church members, both English and Asian, to do this, we realized that it was not worth all the effort we put into the summer team work only to see the contacts lost. That's why we don't have teams these days.

However, we have continued to have volunteers working with us for varying periods of time. This has gone on even though I became severely ill in 1991. This was a shattering blow for us.

18
Surgery

The work in the church and open house continued for the next six years. The encouragements and difficulties I have mentioned continued too. I felt tremendous joy at seeing families putting their trust in the Lord. Sewa and I spent much time in Bible studies and prayer meetings. We felt many of our contacts were going forward spiritually. At the same time, squabbles within the fellowship broke out again at intervals and we lost some families to other churches.

Although I felt physically well in most ways I was suffering from frequent headaches. My doctor thought they were caused by the immense pressure of my work. I was sometimes depressed too. By God's grace I continued with a full-time programme. However, one night the pain in my head was so severe that I had to take some paracetamol before I could go back to sleep. The next night the same thing happened, so I asked Sewa to take me to the doctor. When he did so, I told the doctor that my mother had had a brain tumour and that the pain I had suffered on the previous two nights was not normal. He agreed to send me for a scan.

He made an appointment for me at the hospital but it was for a whole year ahead. When I eventually saw the consultant he didn't think there was anything seriously wrong. However I asked him to give me a scan whatever he thought. It took place a month later.

One Friday afternoon a few days afterwards, the phone rang and I answered it. It was the consultant who began to tell me the scan had revealed some abnormality in my brain. I screamed, 'I told you so! I told you so!' and promptly passed the phone over to Sewa. I was in no fit condition to take in what he said. When Sewa put down the phone, he explained to me that the scan showed a shadow in my brain. I was to go to the Smethwick neurosurgical hospital on Monday morning for an immediate operation.

We went around quietly that evening little realizing that succeeding events were going to turn our lives inside out. The following day Duncan McMann, Crosslinks Area Secretary, phoned about arranging some speaking engagements for us. Sewa told him what happened and he at once expressed great concern. At that point my faith in the Lord didn't waver. I felt sure nothing would go wrong. However in the middle of the night I woke gripped by a terrifying thought. If I had an operation like my mother's, I would be disabled and miss out on all the work I was planning to do. I cried out to Sewa, 'I don't want surgery. I want to die.' 'I won't sign the papers agreeing to an operation and you mustn't either.' I was in a complete panic. I didn't want to live. God had let me down. I was angry with him but I wouldn't tell that to Sewa. I determined to keep the pain inside me, hoping there would be no surgery, determined that they would heal me with tablets or I would die.

Somehow Joan Salt heard that I was going to say, 'No', to surgery, so she gathered a group of people together to pray that I would agree to it after all. Later, I heard that many churches and individual Christians had heard about my plight and were praying for me.

I didn't go to church on Sunday morning but I did in the afternoon. We didn't tell many people there. I sat in the worship meeting and cried, begging the Lord to take this suffering away from me. As we came out of church, Jean Davies, our vicar's wife, put her arms round me and I wept on her shoulder. 'I don't want to end up like my mother and lose my mind and my speech,' I cried. George, who is chairman of the Action Group, and was then a new Christian, overheard and said, 'No, sister, we won't let you end up like your mum.' His words rang in my ears all the time I was in hospital. Later Howell Davies, our vicar, and Duncan and Sewa prayed over me. I felt my courage being built up.

The very suffering I had asked for in order to come close to God was now coming my way. I still determined I wasn't going to have surgery. But on Monday morning as I stepped out of my bedroom a huge, shining throne appeared before me. On it I saw the figure of a man, ablaze with light. People crowded around him. I stood waiting with my head bowed. Then a voice thundered out of the brightness, 'What is the hurry to come back so soon when there is so much work to do on earth?' I felt scared stiff. I knew I was in God's presence. One by one the families in the church went past my eyes. I gazed at some of them and thought of how much they needed help with their difficulties. I couldn't give up on them now. Last of all came Sewa, calm, competent and supportive as always. How could I leave him by saying, 'No', to surgery?

From that moment on I didn't make a fuss. Everything went forward without a hitch. I actually looked forward to the surgery. Ever since then I have believed that what is happening is for the glory of God and I'm going to be completely well one day.

At the hospital everyone was so kind that my fears evaporated. I saw that the other patients in my ward had shaven heads but it didn't worry me. However when I realized the nurses would be shaving off my own long hair, I did feel disturbed. To be one with the Asian women with whom I worked I needed it. I continued to worry about the families in the fellowship. I had grown so close to them that their problems were mine. I hated not being able to stand beside them. This hurt me more than my own problems.

I agreed without a murmur to have the surgery performed, quietly signing the required permission form. On the eve of the operation, Howell and Jean Davies, Duncan McMann and Sewa came to my bedside for holy communion. They also laid hands on me, anointed me with oil and prayed. We all felt our faith had been strengthened. I went to the operating theatre on a Monday in February 1991. The surgery should have taken two to three hours but it actually lasted for six and a half. The tumour covered a third of my brain. Afterwards I stayed unconscious in intensive care for two or three days. When I came round I thought, 'Oh, the surgery is over.' I had no idea it had taken place several days before. I heard friendly voices around me. I opened my eyes and saw Sewa sitting beside my bed. He was gazing at me intently and smiling. I had the impression he had been sitting like that for hours. He said afterwards that God had given him absolute assurance that I would recover. Immediately I said, 'Sewa, I can talk.' I felt so excited, as losing the power of speech had been my greatest fear. It was some time before I realized that the fact that I had come through the operation at all was itself a miracle.

The staff at the hospital were friendly and sympathetic and gave me every encouragement over my progress. I learnt a lot from them and from other patients too. Some of them knew they were dying. I learnt how much such people need love. At the same time, God's love comes through them to others. Geoff Sherwood, another patient, who has since died, was so encouraging to me. He would come from the men's ward and sit by my bed. When I came home, he even telephoned sometimes to see how I was. At first I thought I was going to die too, and I felt so sad that I wouldn't be in this world any more. Then a woman came in who had had a tumour removed twice before. She was extremely upset to be having yet a third operation. I poured out on her all the love of which I was capable through God's enabling. She committed her life to the Lord before she went for surgery. I don't know what happened to her afterwards because we lost contact but I'm sure she was at peace with God. Before I went for surgery I had talked to other patients about the Lord too, and left Christian leaflets in the television room. As soon I could communicate afterwards, I began to talk about Jesus. I loved him so much, I determined that anyone with whom I came into contact should hear about the peace he can give.

So many people came to see me or sent me flowers; and many more, from all over the country, sent their love. It moved me deeply, and I made up my mind that if I lived I would be a changed person. I used to give and give and give to others but if anyone upset me I would keep out of their way and not want to see them. I decided I would contact such people as soon as I felt well enough. I also realized that I was breathing and living work. I had no time for my friends or to enjoy the many gifts God had given me. Now I felt I wanted to have friends outside my work with whom I could relax. I felt I had to some extent made Sewa's life a misery because I insisted so strongly on working that we never had time to sit and enjoy each other. Sometimes we scarcely saw each other for days.

While I lay in bed in hospital I also realized that without suffering I wasn't a complete person. You can sympathize with those who are suffering, you can do things for them but you don't really know what they're going through. I began to say to myself, 'Now I know what my mum must have gone through. The thoughts she must have had before surgery. The thoughts she must have had after surgery.' One of the helpers even came and said to me, 'Give me your hair when they've shaved it off.' How insensitive can a person be? I'm thinking about living or dying and she wants even my hair. I thought of Jesus on the cross and how the soldiers diced for his clothes. I began to understand a little of what he went through.

One day I was told I was to be moved to another hospital. I have no recollection of travelling but I remember waking up in a little room. I felt shattered at the isolation. When Sewa was not there I felt lost, lonely and unhappy. Eventually the sister decided to move me to the main ward. The staff were not as caring or as competent as at the first hospital. As time went on Sewa asked the consultant if I could be moved to another hospital where I could receive more physiotherapy.

When I arrived at the new hospital a sister came to see me. Her voice was like a breath of fresh air. She assured me that she would look after me well and she did. However, though the nurses were attentive and loving, some of them did treat me as though I was handicapped mentally not just physically. They ordered me about like a little child. But the physiotherapists were kind and understanding. I'm still friends with some of them.

Gradually I started taking a few steps holding on to the bars in the gym. The consultant had told Sewa that I might never walk again, so we felt it was a miracle. He had started getting our house reorganized so that I could get around in a wheelchair. He put up rails along the front path that sloped upwards and on both sides of the stairs in the house. He organized a brand new kitchen with low working surfaces that I could use from a wheelchair.

The hospital authorities soon decided I was well enough to go home at weekends. I felt frightened at the thought. Coming back into the world was a big step. The first time, Sewa pushed me home in a wheelchair and took me to a friend's flat for tea. Though it was wonderful to be out with friends again, I felt exhausted afterwards. As my improvement continued, the nurses expected more of me too. Sometimes I felt they asked too much of me in terms of looking after myself. They seemed to think I wasn't trying hard enough and would scold me. In reality what they were asking me to do was beyond my strength at the time. My physiotherapists were encouraging though. Whenever I took an extra step or moved my arm an inch more, they praised me.

In October 1991 after nine months in hospital I came home to live. I would have physiotherapy as an outpatient. I still needed help 24 hours a day so a friend moved into the house. She had her own room but if Sewa was not at home she would spend an hour with me. Sometimes a friend from church would sit with me. However, Sewa did not like to ask for too much help from anyone. He felt he would then have to spend so much time being grateful. Every day he took me for what seemed long walks to try and strengthen my muscles. I was too ill to notice the beauty of the autumn leaves. In any case the sight of my left eye had been affected by the operation. I often didn't recognize people when we met them. When we returned home I felt exhausted. Three times a week Sewa took me for physiotherapy. I made slow progress. I would have liked to have had treatment daily but the staff had too full a programme for that.

I found the outside world discouraging. People have a different attitude to you when you are confined to a wheelchair. On many occasions when we went out, they talked to me as though I couldn't understand what they were saying. This hurt me terribly so I would make an extra effort to walk and hold on to Sewa to avoid being patronized as I sat in the wheelchair.

I had always been an active person. Within a month of coming home I began visiting. I would hold on to the arm of the volunteer we had working with us at the time. I especially went to families I knew were needy. After all, my speech and my brain were perfect and I knew my subject, the Lord Jesus Christ. Nevertheless I did spend long hours at home. Yet I couldn't pray. My mind was focused entirely on my desire to recover. But it didn't seem to be happening. Every day I wished I could die. My inability to love, worship and serve the Lord even drove me to contemplate suicide again and again. Thankfully the fear of the Lord stopped me from taking my life. Once that has been done it cannot be reversed.

When I returned home I expected everything to be the same as when I had left, but my expectations were too high. I was hurting so much more than anyone could see. I looked and sounded quite well, so no one realized how ill I really was. I so wished for a friend who would try and understand my pain, but there was no one. I cried to the Lord for comfort but it did not seem to come. Everyone around was too busy to have time for me. Yet I still felt committed to my work for the Lord. Even in my vulnerability I could not turn away anyone who came for help.

Many friends offered to help but I found it difficult to ring and ask them to come just because I wanted to cry on someone's shoulder. The people who lived with us meant well, but I felt they were laughing at me. Sewa would tell me it was just my imagination. He did his best to look after me and give me love as he still does today. He has never ever complained or moaned, though he has to do the housework, prepare the meals, do the washing and shopping and even clean the toilets. This is the last thing a high caste Indian man would usually be prepared to do. They consider it a job for outcastes.

My love for God had not decreased. Sewa and I would sit and pray together. I would try to read my Bible though not very successfully. I had not been able to do so for a long time. I would hear God's voice assuring me of his love and care for me. Yet often I felt so frustrated by my handicaps that I shut my ears to him. Still I had faith in him and never wavered from the thought that he would make me well.

19

The Ministry Continues

It is now six years since my operation and though I still need help in some ways I am almost independent. Sewa still has to do most of the housework but he never grumbles. I can participate in the work of witnessing to the Lord as though nothing is wrong with me. Even when down in the dumps I continue to trust God. I try to obey him in every area of my life because he has called me to tell the good news to those who have not heard.

Even before I could go out and about much, God brought people to the house who needed to hear about him. More people have given their hearts to the Lord Jesus here than ever did before my illness. It was at this time that one ex-Muslim girl with whom I am still in touch came to Britain for marriage. According to custom she went to live with her in-laws. One week afterwards they threw her out. Because her family were overseas she was destitute. A Christian couple helped her to come to us. She stayed for a year and experienced the love and healing of the Lord in various ways. In the end she gave her life to him. When she gives her testimony she says, 'Sister Narindar said, "The Lord Jesus will give you peace." At first I wouldn't listen to her. But she kept telling me, till one night I said, "Let's pray the prayer and ask Jesus into my heart. I'll never, never go back. Please pray the prayer." ' She's totally illiterate so I said the prayer phrase by phrase and she repeated it after me. She was true to her word. She's never gone back. She was baptized and today she lives in a little flat of her own.

We continued to have other girls in the house too. One mistake we made was to allow someone who had left to return She told us a sob story to persuade us to let her do so, but when she had achieved her wish, she took advantage of us in various ways. In the end, we had to ask her to leave. Since then we have never allowed a girl to come back once she has left. One who was with us couldn't wait to leave. She seemed to think the world outside was full of roses. So we arranged for her to move into her own flat as soon as possible. However, she found herself lonely and unhappy on her own. The bills started coming and she felt under financial pressure. She asked if we would take her back but we refused. We will give them all the help they need in their own place but we won't take them back.

On 1 January 1992, three months after my return from hospital, I received the news that my mother had died. She was sixty and, until she was ill, lived a full life. Although I felt upset I remained quite calm. After all, she was now free of a useless body. I believe she had received Jesus some years before she died. One day when I was in Bible college, I went to see the family after the birth of my brother's first child. My mother and I were together in the sitting room when she went over to the television. She took up a Christmas card that stood on top of it and brought it over to me. She pointed to the picture of the baby Jesus on it and then upwards towards heaven with a smile. I said, 'Mummy, do you understand that he's God.' She nodded and then put the card back. After that she sat down again and pointed to me as if to say, 'I know you believe.' So I told her why I believed and said, 'He forgives sins. Do you want your sins forgiven? Would you like to have salvation?' She nodded again so I said, 'You can't speak but if I pray a prayer will you agree?' Again she nodded so I went ahead and prayed on her behalf, telling Jesus she wanted to accept him as her Saviour. After that she put her hands together and bowed her head as Asians do when acknowledging God. In her last days I heard she spent her time sitting in the gurdwara remembering God in her own way. I believe that, though she was sitting in a Sikh place of worship, she had accepted Jesus and when she was calling upon God she was calling upon him.

In November of the same year Desmond Dansey, who had been such a support to us, had a heart attack and died without recovering consciousness. This was a severe blow to both Sewa and me. Desmond was more than family. He was my teacher in many of the things of God. I felt extremely close to him. He was such a generous person, never ever saying a critical word about anyone. Instead, he encouraged them to go on discovering all the riches that exist in the Lord Jesus Christ. As I wept at his funeral a member of his family came to comfort me and I acknowledged the debt I owed to Desmond for first showing us what Christian service and sacrifice meant.

As if that was not enough, in the summer of 1993 my brother next below me died. This time I felt shattered. Although I would have liked my mother to have lived ten or twenty years longer I didn't feel too distraught because of her age and condition. But I couldn't accept my brother's death. I was, in addition, deeply depressed at the time because of the side effects of a certain medicine I was taking. Such was God's grace that no one who met me knew; but inside I felt dreadful. The news about my brother came on Friday evening. On Sunday morning, I determined not to miss the morning worship. I had seen bereaved Asians keeping away from church for months and months. Sewa said, 'Perhaps you shouldn't go.' However I insisted. Nothing must keep me away from worshipping God. All I wanted was his Spirit to comfort me. No amount of human love could give me the comfort I needed. My brother and I were so close. I know that Asians have close family relationships, but if they had realized the kind of closeness our family had, they would have been astounded. Had I known that my brother was about to die, I would have prayed that I might die in his place. That's how close we were.

Most Asians make an open display of their grief at such times and gain comfort from the sympathetic hugs and demonstrations of love from others. I was different. I wanted to be left alone. Unfortunately, many members of the Punjabi/English Fellowship misunderstood my motives. Perhaps they interpreted my attitude as rejection. Nobody made allowance for the fact that I felt depressed. Depression makes you feel distant from all those around you. Whatever the reason, a number of Asians in the Fellowship didn't understand. They added to my troubles by talking against us. One family even phoned to say, 'We are leaving the church.' Others attacked us viciously, accusing us of all sorts of misdemeanours. Some even shouted and swore at us. We didn't reply. I just visualized Jesus being shouted at during his trials.

Since we began full-time Christian service, we have experienced much suffering and discouragement. I have sometimes felt I was in a pit and no one was coming to get me out. I thought God had deserted me. But then he has held my hand and picked me up. It's been very much like the story of Joseph in the Bible. Every trouble was greater than the last. Often we felt that if we had known before we came into full-time Christian service that there would be so much suffering, struggling and striving we would never have started out on it. Especially after my illness, I felt lost. I couldn't do the one thing I loved most. God was the focus of my life and I couldn't understand why he had put me out of action. But now, looking back, I realize that I have learnt many lessons through my suffering. My trust is only in the Lord Jesus Christ and my total dependency is on him. He rescued me from sin and sickness and taught me, through many situations, something of the extent of human wickedness. Humans are so frail and I have learnt that I cannot trust the best of them too much. At one time I used to fear human beings who were manipulative or deceptive but now I know that only God is to be feared. 'The fear of the Lord — that is wisdom.' (Job 28:28 NIV) But that sort of fear is nothing to worry about. It makes you bow before God in awe and reverence. I know he will never let me down. His trust is all I have left to hold on to.

At times of trouble some Christian friends on whom I had depended left us. Some moved away from Wolverhampton but some just couldn't cope with my illness. But others, even non-Christians, did come and help because they loved us. They visited me when I felt lonely. Some brought us meals. We didn't ask for help. God just kept sending people. He has taught us all through these troubles.

Sewa and I are very much a team. We live to serve God. We always begin the day about 6 a.m. with an hour's Bible study and prayer together. By the time we have finished it is usually 8 o'clock and then I dress. I don't do so earlier because I am energetic and fresh first thing in the morning and I want to give the best time to the Lord. Dressing takes me a long time because of my handicap and Sewa has to help me. Then we have breakfast and by 9.30 a.m. we are ready for the day's work. At night too I try to pray but sometimes I'm so tired I just fall asleep. During the day there is no room for ourselves. We are so busy teaching and helping others. We don't mind because we have surrendered ourselves to the Lord. We are so much alike in this. The more we move forward on the journey of life the more alike we are becoming. I'm amazed how much I'm seeing myself in Sewa spiritually. We both thank God for our togetherness in him.

Another of my great joys is that my father and I have made up after sixteen years. Last time I went to see him we spent three or four hours talking about spiritual things. He had bought a translation of the meanings of the whole Guru Granth Sahib. He is searching. I wish I could spend more time with him because I feel he's much more open than he used to be. He does have a Bible in English and also *Journey into Life*. When I gave him this I said, 'You must spend more time in prayer.' But he said, 'I do read my *gutka* every day.' At the same time I said, 'Have you thought about the prayer I left with you?' He told me he had prayed it, but I think, like me, he has done so without real understanding. Still he did pray it and I believe he is coming closer to God.

We have continued to have volunteers to help with the work. In August 1992 Martina, the daughter of friends, came to us for a year. She is a lovely young woman and after a break of several years she has come back to us again, this time for three years. The other volunteers came from a British organization that sends young people to help in Christian projects. They varied in their attitudes and helpfulness On the whole, they were not as good as the Finnish girls we had had before my illness. One girl was most helpful in driving me around so that I could go visiting within two or three weeks of my leaving hospital. However, she wanted to have her boyfriend in her room and grew angry when I refused permission. Another from a third world country couldn't adjust to either western or Asian culture. She gave us a good deal of trouble and after five weeks we had to ask for her to be moved elsewhere. On the other hand some were good with young people and took a prominent part in activities with them. Others were helpful in relationships between English and Asian members of the church.

We also thank him for the people he is giving us who are like ourselves. Fifty-three Asians were baptized at St Jude's between 1986 and 1993. Not all of them have gone on as we would have liked, but many of them are serving the Lord faithfully. We don't have as many as that in St Jude's church because they have gone all over the country. They are in Manchester, Gravesend, Bradford. You name the cities in Britain where Asians live and our converts are there. We often receive phone calls from them. One in Gravesend regularly sends money for the church. Another in Manchester phones to ask us to send Bible reading notes. One who is still with us here went to Malaysia recently on a month's exchange visit. She was chosen by the diocese. We were so happy that the Lord used her in this way.

We receive immense support from the housegroup God has brought alongside me. The members are very special and such an answer to prayer. I share my troubles with them, knowing they will not gossip but just support me. Sylvia, comes to the Punjabi/English Fellowship especially to help with the children, though she is a busy doctor. The others join us in the service. We serve tea afterwards and English and Asian worshippers join together in fellowship over it.

Another encouragement for us are the eight churches across the country who support us in prayer. They write to us, telephone us, pray for us and give to the work. In the early days they provided us with Punjabi Bibles for Christians who don't read English. We visit them regularly to share news of the work with them. A few of them visit us two or three times a year; usually on Sundays, so that they can join us in the Punjabi/English service. We have occasionally taken members of the Fellowship in the minibus to spend the day with them.

I received yet another blessing directly from God during the traumatic years following my illness. A few months after my mother died I was lying on my bed one afternoon with the curtains at the window drawn back. I lay looking out at the sky and then closed my eyes a little. To my surprise I felt myself going out of my body. The Narindar who got up and started floating out of the window had the same clothes on and looked exactly the same as the Narindar on the bed and yet she was different. As I floated I realized that someone was floating with me on my right side. I knew it was a man but I didn't know who he was. We went up and up into the sky till we came to a large wooden gate that opened downwards. We floated through it and found another sky above our heads. Then we did the same thing all over again and floated into yet a third sky. I saw hills covered with grass. We kept to their left side. On the right, in the distance I glimpsed big, black, monster-like men. Their tongues were dripping with blood. Quickly the man by my side moved us more to the left. Then we came to a stream of clear, bright water. On either side children were laughing, singing and playing on the grass. We left them and moved forward. Then we saw, on the left, men wearing shining silver crowns and cream silk gowns right down to their feet. They were girdled with silver sashes. I looked beyond them and saw another man similarly dressed but with a staff in his hand. He seemed to be keeping the monster-like men away. In a fraction of a second a voice said, 'Who is it?' Another voice replied, 'It's Narindar Mehat, wife of Sewa Mehat.' Then the first voice replied, 'Tell her she is fully well and strong and take her back to earth. She has a lot of work to do, with her husband to help her.' As I was listening to this, a person came to me and seemed to sprinkle something on me. He put a sash round my waist, though he didn't give me a Gown. Then he said, 'Not a crown. I can't give you a crown yet.' As soon as these words were spoken, I floated no more. I was back in my bed. I have never known how or why it happened but from that time I have been much better and stronger. Though my left side is still not quite normal I can walk without anyone's support. I don't even use a stick. The fingers on my left hand are now mobile. I shall consider myself totally healed when I can make chapatis again. And I have every confidence that in a short while I'll be able to do so.

No amount of this world's pleasures gives me the joy that I receive when I sit by someone and they pray a prayer of commitment to Christ. You may say that it is a miracle that I have been healed, but the greatest miracle of all is to see someone acknowledge Christ as their personal Saviour. And then to have the privilege of discipling them. That's wonderful too. Desmond and Enid Dansey taught me that the experience of bringing someone to Christ is like that of a mother going through a great deal of pain but finally giving birth to a baby. It's costly to help someone experience the new birth. It's one-to-one evangelism. But I'm praying that it's the way God will bring hundreds into his kingdom.

As I look back, my heart overflows with thanks to God for what he's done. He brought me from India. He brought Sewa and me together and settled us in Wolverhampton. When I was searching for Christ, he introduced me to the Thursday night fellowship at St Jude's, a church we had no idea existed. Its members gave me love I had never known in Sikh temples. They became a family to us when our own rejected us. God directed me too to the school of his choice where I met needy women and began to reach out to them. Then we experienced the greater joy of seeing some of them come to know him. He led us to start the Punjabi/English Fellowship in our home. At the right time he took us to a Christian college so that we could get to know him and his word in depth. Then he took me through an operation that could have been fatal. Now I'm finding a new life with God more rich than I have previously known.

I wasn't a patient person at all before I became a Christian nor even at first afterwards. I wanted everything yesterday. But I have learnt that the Lord's word, 'Wait', is good for my character. I have also learnt that the Lord delights in who I am before him. It isn't just 'doing', its 'being' with him that matters. Before my illness, I was so busy ministering to others that I didn't go to a house group where my own spirit could receive nourishment. I have also learnt to give and receive love. In my early life I was always receiving from my family. As a Christian I started giving and giving and giving, but I didn't learn to receive. Now I realize that it is important to do both.

God stirred up love for him in my heart when I was very young. But it was many years before I learned to share that love with others. Now I do so all the time. Love is the driving force behind my service to God. It is my reason for living.

APPENDIX

SIKHISM

The Sikh religion into which Narindar was born developed in the Punjab in north-west India, in the late fifteenth century. The Punjab is a region that stretches from snow-capped mountains in the north to fertile green valleys in the south. The climate is extreme: 115° F in May, followed by heavy monsoon rains in July and August. In winter the temperature sometimes drops below freezing point.

Most of the Punjab is good farming land so many Sikhs, like Narindar, are from village backgrounds. But it also includes a number of industrial cities.

Sikhism is practised by about 19 million people worldwide. Few westerners know much about it. This is, perhaps, not surprising as the total number of Sikhs is small, compared with those of other religions, and, until the last forty years, the vast majority lived in one small area of India.

The word 'Sikh' comes from the Punjabi verb *sikhna*, 'to learn'. So a Sikh is a learner or disciple of the Gurus. A faithful Sikh tries to follow their teaching as closely as possible.

Origins of Sikhism: the ten Gurus.

At the same time as Martin Luther was becoming dissatisfied with the teaching of the Roman Catholic church in Europe, in the late fifteenth century, a young man called Nanak felt similarly dissatisfied with the Hindu faith into which he had been born. He also felt disillusioned by the Muslim practices he saw all around him. He therefore began to search for something more satisfying. His search led him to the belief that God is one

and almighty, whereas Hindus believe there are many gods.
Gradually he gathered a group of disciples round him.

Nanak may never have planned to establish a separate religion, but after his death this is what happened. His followers
called him Guru Nanak and succeeding leaders bore that title.
The term 'Guru' means 'teacher'. There were ten successive
Gurus. The second, Guru Angad, invented the Punjabi script
known as *Gurmukhi*.

In the early eighteenth century, the last living Guru, Gobind
Singh, decreed that there would be no more living Gurus. God
would reside in his holy book. Several Gurus, especially the
fifth, Guru Arjan, had collected poems and hymns. He called
the collection the *Ad Granth* ('Ad' means 'first' and 'Granth'
means 'book'). Gobind Singh added other poems and renamed
it the *Guru Granth Sahib*, to emphasize that it was God's word.
The *Mool Mantra*, its opening section, with which Narindar
started her prayers as she was growing up, is said to be Guru
Nanak's first poetic utterance and is a summary of Sikh beliefs.

Guru Arjan also authorized the building of the *Harmindar* at
Amritsar — now the site of the Sikhs' most holy place, the Golden
Temple. This was to be the central place of worship for all Sikhs.
It was a square building with a door in each side to show that it
was open to people of all castes. The present Golden Temple was
built on its site in the nineteenth century. It retains the form of the
Harmindar and is quite small. It is covered in gold leaf, hence its
name. What is said to be the original copy of the *Guru Granth Sahib*
is kept inside and a team of readers reads it aloud continually. The
Golden Temple is situated in the middle of a small lake and
pilgrims approach it across a bridge. They have to step down to
enter the building thus recognizing that they attain a relationship
with God through submission and humility.

A wide paved courtyard surrounds the lake on all four sides.
Around this is a large complex of buildings where all the work
of maintenance and administration of this central shrine of
Sikhism is carried on. There are offices, quarters for the priests
on duty and for pilgrims, a huge kitchen, where hundreds of
chapatis are cooked each day and a communal dining room,
known as the *langar*. Most Sikhs like to visit the Golden Temple
at least once in their lives.

Sikh beliefs

Concept of God
Sikhs believe in one God. He is truth, eternal and self-existent. He is the creator of the universe but he does not sit apart from it. God is in everything and everything is in him. Men and women cannot know or understand him because his greatness is beyond comprehension. Yet people can experience, worship and love him. They can address him in personal terms. This may seem contradictory to some western minds but an Asian may have little difficulty in accepting it.

Concept of humanity
Human beings are the crown of creation. They draw their lives from God. The soul does not die and cannot be destroyed, even by death. God has made men and women moral, value-conscious beings. However, under the pressure of outside influences such as heredity, environment, bad habits or bad friends, the voice of conscience may go unheeded. Men and women are ignorant of their true destiny. Thus they live this life as though it were the only one. Yet God has not left them without hope. He has given them his word, and spiritual teachers to show them eternal truth.

Reincarnation (samsara)
The soul goes through a continuous round of births and deaths, not always as a human being. Human birth is the best of all. Only human beings can distinguish right from wrong. Only they can hear the voice of God. By responding to it repeatedly they can reach a state of permanent bliss in God's presence. Then the soul does not come and go any more. The gurus taught that there are 8.4 million rebirths. But every person does not have to go through all of them. The number can be modified by God's grace.

The grace of God (nadar)
God accepts and blesses a person through his grace. He sets his followers free from the struggle to win appreciation for their actions and transforms them into acts of service. He reveals the meaning of life to those who seek him and gives them a sense

of his presence. There is an element of fatalism about God's grace in Sikhism. We are good or bad in accordance with God's grace. We can only understand spiritual matters if God chooses that we should.

Works (karma)

Until someone relinquishes worldly values, they will be repeatedly reborn. The position in which they find themselves in their present life is, according to the law of *karma*, a consequence of their actions in a previous life. They should aim to achieve freedom from the round of births and deaths. This is only possible when God chooses to set them free. But people are still responsible for their own right conduct. *Karma* is not absolute or inevitable in its effects. God can reduce the number of rebirths if he wishes. But the choice of whether he does so or not is entirely a matter of his will.

Salvation (moksha)

A person needs good spiritual teachers to achieve salvation. However, responsibility for following what they say rests with the individual. People must work out their own salvation through meditating on God's word and name. Eventually they will achieve union with God and the round of births and deaths will cease. However, someone who has turned to Jesus Christ from Sikhism said that no one knows of any Sikh who has achieved union with God.

Meditation (nam simran)

Sikhs should practise this daily. They should try to concentrate their thoughts on God's name. Constant remembrance of God is the way to spiritual peace.

Prayer

Men and women should seek God's blessing on all their activities. But prayer does not reduce their responsibility to work or try to solve their problems themselves. People may pray in their own words but the recitation of set prayers is also important.

Service to others (sewa)

Sikhs should help those lagging behind in spiritual development. They should not cut themselves off by becoming absorbed in their own spiritual progress. Service to others can transform a person's moral and spiritual life. Practical service is also important. People who serve should concentrate on the act of serving and not on its outcome.

The Gurdwara

This is the Sikh place of worship. The word 'gurdwara' means 'the abode of the Guru'. The Sikh flag, the *Nishan Sahib*, flies over every gurdwara or from a flag pole beside it. It is triangular and yellow in colour. The pointed end is finished with a tassel. It stays at full mast throughout the year. In the centre of the flag are three swords which form a black sign known as the *khanda*. The upright two-edged sword in the middle represents freedom and justice. The curved sword on the right represents guidance in spiritual matters, and the one on the left guidance in worldly matters. The circle in the middle, known as the *chakkar*, emphasizes the balance between these two. Before entering a gurdwara, many Sikhs bow to the *Nishan Sahib*. Every *Baisakhi* (spring festival), the old flag is discarded and a new one installed in its place.

The prayer room

This is the most important room in any gurdwara. Pictures of incidents in the lives of the Gurus hang on the walls, but Sikhs do not worship them. The floor is carpeted and covered with white sheets on which the congregation sits, with men on one side of the room and women on the other. Children usually stay with their mothers. The Guru Granth Sahib must be at a higher position than the place where the people sit. In the centre front of the room stands a platform above which hangs a richly decorated wooden or silk canopy. The Granth Sahib stands on cushions on the platform and is covered with a cloth as a sign of respect.

When people come into the gurdwara, they remove their shoes and cover their heads. They walk down a centre strip of carpet to the Granth Sahib where they bow and place offerings of food or money on the rug in front of it. After the service, each member of the congregation is given a little *kara prasad* to eat. *Kara prasad* is a sort of sweet semolina mixture. Then they go to the dining room where they share a meal. Everybody must eat the same food as a symbol of the unity and equality among Sikhs.

Sikhs will be pleased if you want to visit a gurdwara. Learn as much as you can before going. Then contact the secretary and ask for permission to visit. Remember the gurdwara is a special place to Sikhs and behave respectfully. When you reach the entrance take off your shoes and cover your head. Make sure you have no alcohol or tobacco with you. Ask permission if you want to take photographs or make tape recordings. After your visit, a thank you letter will be appreciated.

Worship and Prayer

A Sikh should be consistent in studying scripture and meditating on God. Many Sikhs use the *gutka* (a prayer book containing the choicest parts of the Granth). Sikhs may pray standing, kneeling or sitting, and at any time of day.

Every Sikh should take part in corporate worship. In India there is no weekly holy day, but in Britain services usually take place on Sundays. Sikh worship has no liturgical pattern. It may last fifteen minutes or two hours. The singing of *kirtan* takes up most of the service. This consists of hymns sung to a musical accompaniment.

Sikhs believe manual work is the highest form of worship. No work is unworthy, though some activities are forbidden. These include running a betting club, dating prostitutes, growing or selling tobacco, trading in alcoholic drinks and begging. However, a number of Sikhs have begun to drink since coming to Britain so you may see them in pubs.

Ceremonies

Birth

Sikhism states that parents must welcome every child born, boy or girl, as a gift from God. As soon as possible after a baby's birth

the mother will come to the gurdwara to give thanks. The brief
ceremony includes the giving of the baby's name. The Guru
Granth Sahib is opened at random. The initial letter of the first
word on the left-hand page is that with which the baby's name
should begin. To this is added Singh, meaning 'lion', for a boy,
or Kaur, meaning 'princess', for a girl. Birthday parties are not
part of Indian custom but in Britain many families have taken
over the British custom of remembering a child's date of birth
in this way.

Initiation

Although anyone born of Sikh parents is a Sikh, he or she is not
a full member of the Sikh brotherhood until initiated. This can
happen any time after a person is fourteen. Guru Gobind Singh
introduced this special ceremony on *Baisakhi* Day 1699. A can-
didate should possess the five Ks, accept the doctrines of Sikhism and be attempting to follow the Sikh way of life.

The five Ks are the insignia of the brotherhood that all
initiates, men and women, wear for the rest of their lives. They
include:

Kes — the uncut hair on a person's head or body. Men cover
their hair with a turban, women with a scarf.

Kara — a steel bangle worn on the right wrist.

Kacha — a pair of shorts worn as underwear. They were
introduced, instead of the loose, longer garments
previously worn by men, to allow the wearer freedom in battle.

Kirpan — a steel sword about ten inches long. Most Sikhs now
wear a miniature version round their necks.

Kangha — a small ivory or wooden comb used to keep the
long hair tidy.

Marriage

Most Sikh parents, even in Britain, want to arrange their son or
daughter's marriage. The entire extended family usually takes
part in the organization and expense. A wedding can take place
anywhere where the Guru Granth Sahib is present but usually
happens in a gurdwara.

Funerals

When relations and friends hear of a person's death, they try to reach the family home as soon as possible. Before the cremation the family wash and dress the body and make sure he or she is wearing the five Ks. Anyone who knows the bereaved family even slightly should attend the funeral, so funerals are large affairs. If a Sikh neighbour or work colleague is bereaved, do visit them as soon as possible and attend the funeral.

Friends and relatives continue to visit the mourners for a few days after the funeral. The complete Guru Granth Sahib will be read through over a period of about ten days. When the reading is over, the bereaved and their friends attend the gurdwara to sing and pray for the departed soul. After that, they should not remember the dead person any more because the soul will have been reborn. Sikhs emphasize that men and women should concentrate not on mourning the dead, but on serving the living.

Festivals

The Sikh calendar is based on the phases of the moon so the dates of festivals vary from year to year. In India, festivals often happen on a weekday, but in Britain this is inconvenient, so they are usually held on the Sunday nearest to the actual day.

As many people as possible come to the gurdwara early on the morning of the festival day to listen to the reading of the last five pages of the Guru Granth Sahib. Then follow readings, prayers and hymns about the life of the Guru whose festival is being celebrated. Afterwards there are usually competitions, and, if the weather is suitable, sports with prizes.

Baisakhi (Spring festival)

This usually happens on 13 April, the beginning of the Sikh New Year. It is the day when Guru Gobind Singh initiated the Sikh brotherhood and baptized its first five members.

Diwali (festival of lights)

This festival is popular in Britain, though in India the celebration is usually confined to the Golden Temple (the chief shrine of

Sikhism) in Amritsar. Sikhs illuminate the gurdwara and their own houses with small electric lights or candles. They place them outside, on window sills, above the door and on garden fences. In places where many Sikhs live, the streets are lined with hundreds of lights.

Gurpurbs
These festivals remind Sikhs of important events in the lives of the Gurus. The birthday of Guru Nanak is celebrated in November, and that of Guru Gobind Singh in December. The martyrdom of the Fifth Guru, Arjan, is remembered in June or July.

Some Sikh characteristics

1. Sikhs emphasize the family and reject the asceticism common in Hinduism. Hindu holy men and women spend much time alone and subject themselves to rigorous self discipline often depriving themselves of such generally accepted necessities as food, clothes and shelter. Sikhs count fellowship with other believers the touchstone of their faith. Sikhs should live in the world. Service to one's fellowmen is the mark of holiness. This has resulted in considerable social progress. For example, women are somewhat freer than in most Hindu areas of India and farmers are often willing to try out new farming methods, instead of clinging stubbornly to traditional methods.
2. Sikhs take their duty towards the community seriously. They have founded hospitals and orphanages and have a general sense of industry and responsibility. Members of a high class family may sweep the ground or wash the dishes at their place of worship. A devout Sikh tithes.
3. They are hospitable and will go out of their way to make a stranger feel welcome. So we needn't be nervous about going to visit Sikh acquaintances.
4. They are loyal, especially to fellow worshippers and friends.
5. They are independent and democratic, all equal members of a brotherhood. This spirit of independence means they put a premium on being well-organized and efficient.

6. They are often physically courageous. Their ancestry and history of persecution has developed in them a warrior strain which can make them tenacious and determined.
7. At the same time, they can be adaptable and flexible when the need arises. They will make the most of any circumstances and adjust accordingly, since they are fatalists, believing that what happens to them is God's will.

Some Other Characteristics

The Turban

The turban was originally introduced to identify a person as a Sikh. A Sikh man should wear one, even if bald-headed. A turban consists of a piece of cloth about 5.5 m long and 45 cm wide. A well-tied turban can be worn several times before it loses its shape and needs washing. Under the turban, the long hair is tied into a top knot.

A small boy's hair is plaited and kept in place with ribbons, so it is sometimes impossible to distinguish them from girls. When a boy is a little older, he graduates to a top knot and, later, to a turban.

Work habits

The Sikh community in Britain has proved itself adaptable. Most families were landowners in the Punjab, but here they have become labourers, skilled workers, businessmen, lawyers, etc. Most Sikhs prefer to work for themselves rather than be employed by someone else. As soon as they have amassed enough capital, many buy businesses: garages, warehouses, factories and shops. Others become insurance agents, driving instructors, teachers, policemen. The list is endless.

Role of women

In theory, men and women are regarded as equal; in practice it is not fully so. A mother is traditionally the queen of the household and the father the breadwinner, but in Britain, many women also go out to work. On the whole, women play a subordinate role in the Sikh community.

Community and family

Sikhs have kept their distinctiveness as an ethnic group to a large extent and maintained a strong sense of identity. The emphasis on community and family values has been a major factor in this. Sikhs should have one lifelong partner. The doctrine of *sewa* has instilled in Sikhs a strong sense of honour and loyalty to one's family, to those from the same village in the Punjab, to friends, to the entire Sikh community. These values are more important than one's personal welfare. Even very westernized Sikhs respect their parents and help needy relatives. They often finance the education of younger members of the extended family. They cherish its emotional support and take pride in fulfilling their duty to it.

Teenage boys and girls are usually kept strictly apart. Punjabi culture has no concept of boy and girl friendships that do not involve sex and view sex before marriage as extremely reprehensible. Christian men and women who want to be a good witness for the Lord should never initiate conversations with the opposite sex, unless they know the family very well indeed, and are sure they understand western ways.

Family honour (izzat)

This plays a large part in the life of a Sikh. Izzat is the respect society places on individual family groups when they behave in culturally acceptable ways. A family protects its own *izzat* in every possible way by trying to see that all members live up to it. The 'bad' behaviour of children can detract from family *izzat*. Other members of the community will criticize the family for not enforcing firm discipline. Personal prestige should be subordinated to the communal approval of the group. A son may have to forego the career of his choice if his father feels it would detract from the family *izzat*.

Conflict between the generations

In spite of group loyalties such conflict does exist. Older Sikhs worry because their young people are absorbing the principle of individualism, prized in the West but alien to eastern thought. This sometimes leads to clashes between children and their families. Though most work through these without outside help, a few young people do appeal to social workers for assistance. This sometimes aggravates the situation. A western social worker will usually uphold the value of individualism and fail to understand the Punjabi concept of group honour.

Despite this, rebellion and disobedience are less of a problem among Punjabi than English families. Delinquency and crime are also less common. Parents encourage their children to work hard at school and supervise homework and free time carefully. Some teach their children about the Sikh faith at home. Others look to the gurdwara to do this.

Recent political history of the Punjab

Since the 1970s, many Sikhs have been asking for changes in the provincial government tantamount to independence. Those prepared to use force found a leader in an extreme Sikh called Jarnail Singh Bhindranwala. In the early eighties unrest grew and Bhindranwala was accused of organizing violent opposition to the government and plotting its overthrow. He withdrew to the Golden Temple complex, made it his headquarters and began to stockpile arms. Months of growing tension followed until, in June 1984, the Indian Army, under a Sikh officer, stormed the Temple in what became known as Operation Blue Star. A two-day battle followed. Bhindranwala and a number of his followers were killed.

But this was not the end of the troubles. Most Sikhs were outraged at the desecration of their most holy shrine. Violence followed all over the Punjab and the Indian government was unable to contain it. In October 1986 Mrs Gandhi, India's Prime Minister, who had ordered operation Blue Star, was assassinated in Delhi by two of her own bodyguard, who were Sikhs. Riots followed in Delhi, and even abroad where there are large numbers of Sikhs. In India many Sikhs and Hindus were killed or injured. A large number were arrested. Shooting and killing continued in the Punjab. Even today some unrest still occurs and the future of the Punjab is uncertain.

Many Sikhs overseas are worried that the violence in the Punjab gave the world a tarnished image of Sikhism. Nevertheless, some of them would like to see Sikhs in the Punjab having more control over their own affairs. Most Sikhs in Britain are concerned about the fate of the Punjab. The majority have relatives there and worry about their safety. It is good to be aware of this when talking to Sikh friends.

In conclusion

Over 40 per cent of the Sikh community in Britain were born here. They may never have visited the Punjab, yet describe themselves as Punjabis. White British people may not regard them as British. Most British born Sikhs are proud to belong to the Sikh community. It gives them a sense of pride, identity and self respect. If you have a Sikh neighbour, or work colleague, you can expect them to be polite, hardworking and caring.

Aisha my Sister
Christian Encounters with Muslim Women in Britain
Editor: Sally J. Sutcliffe

Does your image of Muslim women go beyond the veil?

In *Aisha My Sister* over twenty Christian women from a variety of cultural backgrounds, some former Muslims, describe the joys and surprises of making friends across ethnic and religious barriers in Britain. From personal insights and experience, this book looks at making friends, encountering Islamic ways of life and the response of the church to its Muslim neighbours.

Packed with plenty of practical suggestions, this is a resource and study book for Christian women of all walks of life who want to reach out to their female Muslim friends, neighbours and colleagues.

"Sally Sutcliffe's practical experience takes you into many Muslim homes . . . places where you empathize, sympathize, drink tea and make friends. Evangelization of Muslim peoples, and in particular of Muslim women, only happen one at a time – when Aisha becomes your sister! . . . Highly recommended." – Pradip Sudra, Alliance of Asian Christians

Sally Sutcliffe has worked with Interserve's Ministry among Asians in Britain (MAB) since 1992. She is presently working as Communications Consultant.

ISBN 1-900507-44-7

Sadhu Sundar Singh
A Biography of the Remarkable Indian Holy Man and Disciple of Jesus Christ
Phyllis Thompson

Barely hours before he intended to take his own life, the young Sundar Singh had a vision of Jesus Christ. Immediately the emptiness and despair that had filled his heart was lifted, and his search for inner peace was over.

Despite opposition and rejection at home, he soon knew that he had to share his faith throughout the towns and villages of India, and beyond into the dangerous mountain regions of Tibet.

ISBN 1-85078-099-4

Patricia St John Tells Her Own Story

"Quiet, unassuming, self-effacing, yet with a wonderful twinkle in her eye, Patricia was one of the greatest saints I have ever met. Instinctively, in her presence, you knew you were being given a fresh glimpse of the radiance, dignity and graciousness of Christ himself, whom she loved so much."
Michele Guiness, Writer and Broadcaster

"It has been a revelation to read of her involvement in the spread of the gospel, all she has done through relief work with Global Care . . . and specially her courage when, as a young missionary, she went to live alone in a Muslim town."
Phyllis Thompson, Author of *Sadhu Sundar Singh*

ISBN 1-85078-279-2

Until the Day Breaks

The Life and Work of Lilias Trotter, Pioneer Missionary to Muslim North Africa

Patricia St John

As a young woman who had just turned down a promising career as an artist to serve Christ, Lillias Trotter's missionary call started as 'a strange yearning' love for those who were in the land of the shadow of death'. Despite being refused by a missionary society on health grounds, she was soon sailing into the port of Algiers to begin an evangelistic work that was totally unconventional for a European woman of the day.

ISBN 1-85078-077-3